I HAD A

Ball

My Friendship with Lucille Ball

MICHAEL Z. STERN

iUniverse, Inc.
Bloomington

I Had a Ball
My Friendship with Lucille Ball

iUniverse books may be ordered through booksellers or by contacting:

iUniverse
1663 Liberty Drive
Bloomington, IN 47403
www.iuniverse.com
1-800-Authors (1-800-288-4677)

Because of the dynamic nature of the Internet, any Web addresses or links contained in this book may have changed since publication and may no longer be valid. The views expressed in this work are solely those of the author and do not necessarily reflect the views of the publisher, and the publisher hereby disclaims any responsibility for them.

Any people depicted in stock imagery provided by Thinkstock are models, and such images are being used for illustrative purposes only.

Certain stock imagery © Thinkstock.

ISBN: 978-1-4502-8731-9 (sc)
ISBN: 978-1-4502-8730-2 (dj)
ISBN: 978-1-4502-8729-6 (ebook)

Library of Congress Control Number: 2011900968

Printed in the United States of America

iUniverse rev. date: 5/31/2011

Acknowledgments

There are many people who have helped me throughout my life. Since this is the only book that I plan on writing, I have to take this opportunity to mention a whole bunch of folks who inspired me.

This might sound like I won an Emmy or an Oscar, so brace yourself. Here's my speech ...

I first and foremost would like to thank my two wonderful parents, Beverley and Norman. Without their guidance, love, and understanding, I would not be the person that I am today. I think of them every day. I miss them very much. I always wanted them to be proud of me, and I know that I've succeeded!

I'd also like to thank my brother, Jeffrey and my sister Maxine for always putting up with me during my entire Lucy phase which, I'll admit, still kind of goes on to this day!). I thank My Brother in Law Ricky, and Sister in Law Bonnie who both have brought much joy to the family.

And to all my relatives: Aunt Rose, Uncle Joe, and Aunt Esther; my nephews, nieces, and great-nieces; my first, second, third, and fourth cousins—all of whom will buy a copy of my book—I thank you!

And to my Lucy-world family and friends—Lucie Arnaz Luckinbill, Desi and Amy Arnaz, Elisabeth Edwards, Wanda Clark, Frank Gorey, Tom Watson, Richard Brock, Stuart Shostak, Garret Boyajian, George Ridjaneck, Rick Carl, Suzanne LaRusch, Keith Thibodeaux, Diane Vincent, Gregg Oppenheimer, and all my friends at the Lucy-Desi Center in Jamestown—thank you for allowing me to be a part of your family. Your support means everything to me.

And thanks to my former bosses who have helped me get to where I am today. A special thank-you to Donna Martin, Chris Cavarozzi, and Larry Einhorn.

I also want to thank Rich deMichele for hiring me on the *Dr. Phil* show.

And a big thank-you to Dr. Phil McGraw, who, after I had been on the job for just a few weeks, called me and said, "You're hitting the ball out of the park."

To all the people who I work with, I thank you for your friendship.

And thank you to those who helped me put this book together. The folks at iUniverse—

To Rhoda Shapiro, who gave me my words when I couldn't come up with them. To my longtime friend Darin Plotnick, who refreshed many of my memories and stories. And to Kevin Gentry, who furnished me with pictures of myself and Lucy when I thought no one had them.

To my friends from *A* to *Z*, thank you...Andrew, Brad, Craig, David, Eileen, Florence, Gilmore, Henry, Irene, Janet, Keith, Lance, Mark, Nicole, Peter, Rhonda, Scott, Tobi, Valerie, and Zachary. Since I am on a roll, I like to add Barbara, Bruce, Charlene, Chris, Christian, Dana, Kayla, Ken, Marcia, Marilyn, Michael, Peggy, Shelly, Stephanie and Steve. I think I now have added all including all The Awerkamps, The Rosens, The Millers and The Shabbot group.

Whew. And that's only just the beginning of the list of people I would like to thank!

Love to all,

Michael

CHAPTER 1

This is the hardest part of the book to write.

How do I even begin to tell the story of a young boy who grew up in Canada and moved to Hollywood, California, where he would later become friends with one of the biggest and brightest television personalities of all time, Lucille Ball?

Oh, wait. I just did.

Although Lucy is no longer here, the memory of her warm and free-spirited presence still lingers in my mind. Not a day goes by that I don't think or talk about Lucy. Her impact on my life is undeniable. I used to eat, drink, sleep, and watch Lucy. If Lucy said on TV to do something, I'd rush to do it, without a moment of hesitation. If my parents told me to do the same thing, I'd argue until I was blue in the face. In my eyes, Lucy could do no wrong. With her wit and enthusiasm, she lived life without limitation, embracing the capricious nature of it with all of herself.

I lived in Winnipeg for the first six years of my life. From what I can remember, it was an enjoyable and carefree time, a time in which I was free to explore and create and imagine.

At one point of my young life in Canada, we moved to a small city sixty miles west of Winnipeg called Portage La Prairie. Full of nature and open spaces, the area offered the perfect environment in which my two older siblings and I could play. There was a nearby lake that we spent a great deal of time at. In the winter, I would go out into the snow with my brother, Jeffrey (seven years older than me), and my sister, Maxine (five years older). During the summers, we spent all our time at the local Dairy Queen.

Back in Canada, there was no shortage of family gatherings. I had a slew of aunts, uncles, and cousins whom I saw on a regular basis. Whether it was having meals together or hanging around my grandfather's grocery store and lunch counter, we were a tightknit bunch.

On August 1, 1967, my parents, siblings, and I gathered up our belongings and headed to Hollywood! Well, more like the San Fernando Valley part of the Los Angeles suburbs. My Aunt Anne and Uncle Bernard, from my mother's side of the family, were already living in Southern California, and my parents thought it would be a good idea to move close to them.

Since I had never been to Los Angeles, I didn't know what to expect. We arrived in the palm-tree-laced town on August 6, which just so happened to be Lucy's birthday. Although I wasn't aware of it at the time, my path toward Lucy had just begun.

The first time I ever saw Lucille Ball, it was on the big screen in the 1968 film *Yours, Mine and Ours*. The film starred Lucy, Henry Fonda, Van Johnson, and Tom Bosley and was written by Lucy's TV writers, Bob Carroll Jr. and Madelyn Pugh Davis. I was only seven years old when the movie came out. At the time, I was back in Winnipeg for a family gathering. My parents basically forced my sister, Maxine, to take me to the movie theater for the afternoon.

My sister was always the one who ended up taking me to the movies. I still recall the first movie she took me to when I was five years old. It was the 1966 Herman's Hermits (a Beatles-type singing group) film, *Hold On!*

Since I was a very hyper child, it was quite a challenge for my sister to keep me calm and in my seat during any movie. With my boundless energy and short attention span, I would often get up and run around the theater.

However, with *Yours, Mine and Ours*, it was different. There was something about this one that stood out from the others I had seen. The forty-foot-tall, red-haired lady on the screen had my complete focus. Her radiance and charisma had me hooked. Once the movie finished, I had already made up my mind to go see it again. I begged my parents to take me back a few days later. *This request from a kid who could not keep still for the life of him.*

A few months later, I was watching TV in our Los Angeles apartment and a show called *I Love Lucy* came on. From exhilarating start to climactic finish, I simply could not stop laughing.

"You know, that's Lucille Ball," my aunt Anne told me after the show was over. "She's that same lady who was in *Yours, Mine and Ours*."

I was completely puzzled for a moment. Lucy Ricardo and Helen North had two completely different personalities. It never struck me that it was the same woman playing both roles! Perhaps it was the fact that the movie was in color and the television show was in black and white that threw me completely off. I wasn't quite sure. But what I was sure about was that at that moment, *a new Lucy fan came to be.*

*　　　*　　　*

For the next few years, I made it my mission to watch Lucy every night at 7:00 p.m. At the time, there was nothing I looked forward to more. *I Love Lucy* was one of my favorite shows. Every time I sat down to watch it, the walls of the apartment living room seemed to expand with the promise of newness. Television transported me to another place, one that was rich with humor, intrigue, and character.

During that time, I watched a lot of other shows. Shows like *The Patty Duke Show*, *Please Don't Eat the Daisies*, *The Mothers-in-Law*, *Family Affair*, *Green Acres*, *The Brady Bunch*, and *The Partridge Family*. My parents even let me stay up late on Monday nights to watch Lucy's third sitcom, *Here's Lucy*, which started in 1968 and ran until 1974. Although it was a bit challenging for me to wrap my mind around Lucy Ricardo and Lucy Carter being the same person, nevertheless, I enjoyed watching Lucy immensely. *Here's Lucy* was just another opportunity to witness her limitless genius.

*　　　*　　　*

I had a childhood friend named Holly who lived right across the street from me. We shared a closeness that was unparalleled in any of the other friendships I had. We spent hours playing and getting into all kinds of trouble with one another, inside and outside of school.

Then one day Holly and her family moved away, leaving me absolutely heartbroken. I needed a new friend.

But who could replace Holly?

I looked around and found no answers.

However, it just so happened that the new people who moved into Holly's house filled that void for me completely.

My new neighbors were Marcia and John Brenner, a warm and welcoming couple who had just recently gotten married. When they bought the house, little did they know that *I* was included in the sale!

I spent countless hours at their home. Marcia and John had a love of television as well, and they often invited me to watch all kinds of shows with them. Marcia even gave me all of her celebrity magazines in which Lucy graced the pages. And thus began my Lucy collection. I would immediately cut Lucy's images out of the magazines, careful not to make any crooked edges. Once I was finished, I would staple the pictures to the walls of my bedroom. Pretty soon, my bedroom walls were completely plastered with Lucy pictures.

After some time, I made an incredible discovery: Marcia had a connection to Lucy. Marcia's mother, Peggy, worked for a man named Ben Kanter, who was the saxophonist for the *Here's Lucy* band on Thursdays, the day the show filmed in front of a live studio audience. Upon learning of this connection, pure adrenaline pumped through my insides. *This was my way in.*

Marcia reached out to Peggy, who reached out to Ben. And after just one conversation, Peggy was able to talk him into getting me tickets to the show. When I heard the news, I could hardly believe it. The luminous actress I had spent the last few years watching on my television was now going to be in the exact same room with me. It was too surreal for words.

On Thursday, October 28, 1971, I went to my very first filming of *Here's Lucy*. Luckily, my parents were cool enough to let me skip school that day, as they knew how important this was to me. It was a once-in-a-lifetime event, one that I would never forget.

We drove to Universal Studios, home of *Here's Lucy*, and arrived at noon. My brother, Jeffrey, was fortunate enough to be the one to escort me. We walked right up to Guest Relations. As we approached the desk, I took a couple of quick breaths, trying to cool my nervousness.

A few days ago, Peggy had informed me that the minimum age to see the show was twelve. At that point, I wasn't even eleven yet.

"If they ask you how old you are, just tell 'em you're twelve," Peggy advised me

I nodded, confident that I would make it through with no problems.

But now, standing there in front of the desk, that confidence was miles away. In my head, I started to doubt myself. I thought it might be too good to be true. *What if I didn't make it in to see Lucy?*

As the gentleman at the desk looked over at me, I adjusted my shoulders and straightened my posture, in an attempt to look mature. It must have worked, because he never asked me my age. He just gestured toward the food court and told us to wait there until we were called inside.

We sat down and went about the business of waiting. I shifted in my seat, eager to get into the studio.

Then, after what seemed to be hours (although it was probably more like twenty minutes), the voice of the gentleman from Guest Relations sounded over a loudspeaker: "If you're on the guest list for *Here's Lucy*, please line up by the tram."

Before the man could even get the words out, I had leaped off my seat, ready to go.

Forty of us guests piled into a studio tram and were zipped over to Stage Twenty-Four in about five minutes. As we pulled up, my eyes immediately went to the massive posters of Lucy, Lucie Arnaz, and Gale Gordon that were hanging outside the studio. Jabs of excitement went up and down my spine.

We were then ushered into the soundstage. It was empty, except for all of the guests. An usher asked for our names again, and we were efficiently escorted to our reserved seats, which were in the corner of the far left section, facing the stage. When we arrived there, we found pieces of masking tape with the name "STERN" on them attached to our seats. Those seats belonged *to us.*

The rest of the studio audience was divided into three sections. Once we had settled into our seats, about two hundred other people were then ushered into the studio. (I later learned that every Thursday afternoon, people who went on the studio tram tours had the chance to win seats to see *Here's Lucy*. One lucky tram was picked at random and then invited to see the show.)

After the general public was seated, about twenty people from backstage were escorted to their seats. Lucy's mom, DeDe, was one of them, along with actor/comedian Jesse White, who sat behind us. (At the time, I recognized him as the Maytag repairman from the TV commercials, but I didn't know his name. He also guest starred in countless TV shows.)

Lucy's orchestra came out to perform on a platform that was located on the far right side of the audience. Orchestra leader Marl Young entertained us with a flurry of magnificent tones and chords for the next twenty minutes. He then introduced announcer Roy Rowan, who had been with Lucy from the very beginning of *I Love Lucy*.

After chatting for a few minutes with the audience, Roy introduced Lucy's husband, Gary Morton, who told a series of jokes and stories for five minutes. While he was up there, Gary also mentioned that Lucy was very excited, as her special guest the week before had been her longtime friend Vivian Vance, who played the character Ethel Mertz from *I Love Lucy*. He went on to say that today she was pleased to have another one of her longtime friends present. His name was Bob Cummings, and he was really famous in the fifties and sixties. I had no idea who he was at the time, but found out later that he was the star of *Love That Bob* and *The Bob Cummings Show*. The shows weren't in reruns. He had also guest starred in an episode of the *Lucy-Desi Comedy Hour* show called "The Ricardos Go to Japan."

Gary went on to introduce the cast. I sat up straight in my seat, craning my neck, preparing to get a glimpse of all the performers. First out was Lucie Arnaz, who played Lucy's daughter Kim. Sporting a big and beautiful smile, she took a gracious bow as the audience cheered.

Next up was Gale Gordon. Gary introduced Gale as Lucy's good luck charm. He told us that Gale had worked with Lucy on radio and every series that Lucy had ever done. Now he was playing Uncle Harry, Lucy's boss and brother-in-law. He came out, took a bow, and performed a perfect cartwheel as he left the stage.

After Gale disappeared from view, Gary turned back to the audience and took a deep breath. *It was time to introduce Lucy.*

After dazzling us with a glowing introduction, Gary called out Lucy's name. Before he could even get her entire name out, the audience was already cheering and getting on their feet. Then in an instant, Lucy burst out from behind a curtain on center stage.

Lucy's penetrating blue eyes scanned the audience. From the looks of the tremendous smile that filled her face, she was thrilled to be receiving a standing ovation (even though she probably had received hundreds in the past). The *Here's Lucy* theme music started to play at full volume, filling the air with energy and excitement.

With her red hair ablaze, Lucy engaged the audience with all of herself. First, she ran to the section I was in and started blowing kisses and waving. I looked out at her, waving back, my eyes large and my breath suspended. After all this time, I was actually getting to see Lucy outside the confines of my television set. I could hardly believe that she was a mere forty feet away.

For a ten-year-old kid like me, this meant the world.

Within a few seconds, Lucy had turned from our section and was already headed toward the other end of the stage, where she continued to blow kisses and wave. After that, she headed back to center stage, where Gary handed her a microphone.

I, along with the rest of the audience, sat back down, eager to hear what Lucy had to say. She introduced her mom, DeDe, who she told us was at every filming. She also introduced her friend Jesse White. As she continued to speak, I sat there completely still, not moving a single muscle. I was afraid that if I did, I would somehow miss something that Lucy was saying.

At the end of her quick speech, Lucy looked out at the audience and beamed. "I think we have a great show for you this afternoon. Thanks so much for being here!"

With that, Lucy handed the microphone back to Gary, and all the stagehands and cameramen got to their posts to start filming "Lucy's Punctured Romance," which was written by Fred S. Fox and Seaman Jacobs.

As Lucy left the stage, stagehands revealed the center set by moving apart five curtains on rollers. It was the living room of the Carters, the place where the characters of Lucy and Kim lived. Sitting on the sofa was Mary Jane Croft, who Gary introduced to everyone in the audience.

Mary Jane was a semi-regular on the show. She played Betty Ramsey, the Westport neighbor on *I Love Lucy*. On *The Lucy Show*, she played Mary Jane Lewis, Lucy's neighbor in California. And now on *Here's Lucy*, she was again playing her friend Mary Jane.

I was ecstatic to see her because I remembered her from all the other Lucy shows. Not only that, she was one of my favorite television characters.

Leaning toward the audience, microphone in hand, Gary set the scene with his smooth and articulate manner, telling us that it was a Saturday afternoon in the Carter home.

As the show began to unfold, I sat there mesmerized. Magic was being made before my very eyes. I locked in, transfixed by every moment, every gesture, every line. I did not take a single detail for granted.

In the episode, Lucy met a handsome bachelor (Bob Cummings), and the fire of romance was lit between them. However, the Carters' milkman told Kim that the man drank a lot and had a bevy of girls visiting his home. Kim and Uncle Harry schemed to save Lucy from herself by making Bob think Lucy was a deaf, alcoholic, hot-pepper-eating harlot.

The actual filming took less than ninety minutes. During the breaks, Lucy would look out at the audience and crack jokes. Everyone was delighted by her humor and spontaneity.

After the last scene, Lucy took the microphone from Gary and introduced the entire cast, asking them to take their bows. Then she thanked us for coming and told us to drive safely.

As we filed out of the studio, I noticed the stage crew going over to fix the Carters' living room front door. (In the last scene, firefighters had come in and had to break down the door.)

That was the last glimpse I got of the *Here's Lucy* set before stepping back out into the world.

To this day that is one of the greatest highlights of my life.

The STERN FAMILY August 6, 1968 (L-R) brother Jeffrey,
mom Beverley, dad Norman, sister Maxine and me

*Making my brother, Jeffrey, sleep in this room
was no easy task ... I had no problem!*

CHAPTER 2

The next day I went back to school and proudly informed all my fellow classmates that I had not been sick, but had, in fact, attended a filming of *Here's Lucy*. My peers heard these words and simply looked back at me, disinterest in their eyes.

Not the reaction I was expecting at all.

Perhaps it wasn't cool to like Lucy at the time? Or maybe they were just upset that I had a day off and they didn't. Whatever the reason, I didn't have time to reflect on it. My teacher, Mrs. Foley, was extremely excited for me, as she knew how much I loved Lucy.

I was still in a daze from the day before. Bits of the studio taping replayed in my mind. I wanted to relive it over and over.

Four months later—on Monday, February 7, 1972—the episode that I saw being filmed finally aired. I watched the show very closely and discovered that it was as funny on television as it was being there. Nothing had changed, and as far as I remembered, nothing had been cut. It gave me such a sense of pure elation to know exactly what was going to happen before it aired. I felt as if I was *in* on something.

It was a big deal in our household. My entire family sat around the television that night, eating popcorn that my dad made.

Months later, I received a special phone call from Peggy.

"My boss is going to appear in a *Here's Lucy* episode, and he was able to get extra tickets to the show," she told me.

I held my breath, waiting for her to say the words I hoped she would. "Yeah?"

"Do you want to be my guest?"

"Yes!" I replied, squeezing the phone in my hands.

I later discovered that this filming of *Here's Lucy* was going to be a special one, featuring Donny Osmond of the Osmond Brothers singing group. At the time, Donny, just fourteen years old, was a huge star in the recording industry. He had hit songs like "Puppy Love," "The Twelfth of Never," and "Young Love" blasting the radio waves, sweeping everyone up with their lyrics and youthful energy.

Years later, Donny would team up with his younger sister, Marie, and they would go on to have a huge duet career, which eventually led to their own prime-time variety show.

On June 15, Peggy picked me up, and off we drove to Universal Studios. We walked up to Guest Relations, just as my brother and I had done the last time. But there was one big difference. This time it seemed that about 90 percent of the studio audience was on the guest list.

As we arrived at Stage Twenty-Four, I saw a huge group, consisting of mostly young girls, waiting outside the studio entrance. Donny's brothers, who were not in the episode, were outside taking photos with fans and signing autographs. I hadn't yet begun to collect autographs, so I didn't even think about asking. (In the next few years, I became a very large autograph collector and regretted not getting the Osmond brothers to sign that day.)

We waited about twenty minutes before we were able to enter the studio. Once we got inside, Peggy and I made our way to our seats which, to my delight, were toward the center of the second row.

The second row. I simply could not believe my luck.

The first row was taken up by the Osmond brothers and their parents. Marie was the only one who wasn't present at the filming. (Recently, I saw Marie at a *Dr. Phil* taping. I asked her why she hadn't made it to the taping of that episode, and she told me that she had been recording her first album.)

I settled back into my seat, eager for what the afternoon would bring. I knew the show was about to start when Marl Young started to play the same songs he had played when I was there eight months earlier. When he was finished, Roy Rowan did the same introductions, and Gary Morton did all the same jokes. I didn't completely comprehend it at the time, but I realized later that this is normal practice in the TV-taping world, where it's assumed that you are playing to a different and fresh audience each week. (I now do the closing for the *Dr. Phil* show. After Dr. Phil leaves the audience, I say the same three jokes at every show.)

Just before Gary introduced Lucy, he introduced her daughter, Lucie, who came out and bowed. Since Gale had a rare week off for this episode, he wasn't present.

After Lucie left the stage, Gary mustered up all his gusto and introduced Lucy. But instead of springing out and running from one end of the stage to the other, Lucy walked very slowly to center stage, a slight skip in her footing.

Since the last time I had seen her, she had broken her leg in Aspen while skiing. Someone had run into her on the slopes. Because of her injury, many episodes were written about her skiing accident, a few of which even had Lucy in a wheelchair. Her leg cast had just been removed a few weeks earlier.

But Lucy's slow gait did nothing to cool the reception of the audience. As usual, the entire studio was thrilled to see her, and we expressed our appreciation with loud clapping and cheering.

After Lucy joined Gary onstage, they proceeded to talk to the studio audience, and even answer some questions.

A gentleman from the middle section asked Lucy if Desi was ever going to return to the show. Before Lucy could answer, Gary put on a confused expression and asked, "Which Desi?"

Lucy gave Gary a playful shove that nearly knocked him off the stage. People in the audience chuckled.

Lucy turned to the gentleman who had asked the question, answering with a light-hearted tone, "We would love for Desi to return to *Here's Lucy*, but we can't afford him. He's off doing movies."

After all the questions were answered, it was time to get the show on the road.

When the curtain opened for the first scene, I could see that it was set at the far right of the stage, where the Unique Employment Agency set had been the last time. Most times, three sets could have been used during the course of one filming.

Usually the Carter living room was in the middle of the stage. To the left was the Carter kitchen or the Unique Employment Agency, where Lucy and Uncle Harry worked. On the other side of the Carter living room was what was called the swing set, which was the set of the week that was needed for that week's episode. One week it might have been a ski lodge; the next, a diner or a nightclub. This time, the set was perfectly staged for a nightclub.

Gary announced that playing the part of Lucy's niece, Patricia, was the talented young actress Eve Plumb, from the hit television series *The Brady Bunch*, which I had heard was actually inspired by *Yours, Mine and Ours*.

Eve had been playing Jan Brady, the middle daughter, for the five-year run of the series. Since I watched *The Brady Bunch* every Friday night and knew it quite well, I was beyond thrilled to see Eve Plumb. I think this was the only time in the *Here's Lucy* series that we heard that Lucy had other family members. Therein lies the magic and power of television. A family member can be born at any time!

In the episode's story line, Kim (Lucie) was able to get tickets to see a

Donny Osmond concert. Patricia (Eve Plumb) was a huge fan of Donny's. After Donny's nightclub show was over and everybody but the Carters had left the nightclub, Lucy asked the maître d' if she could have a few souvenirs.

As the maître d' was a friend of Lucy's daughter, he responded, "Since you are Kim's mother, yes."

Wasting no time at all, Lucy proceeded to take the sugar cubes, matches, ashtrays, place mats, menu … and even the flowers and vase! It was an amusing scene that had the audience howling with laughter.

The show went fairly smoothly. There were just a couple of scenes, including the opening scene, that was done twice. As all the scenes in the Bob Cummings' episode I had seen were only shot once, it was incredibly enjoyable to actually see a scene get shot a second time.

"Now that you know where the jokes are, be sure to laugh in the exact same spot you laughed the first time," Gary told us, microphone in hand, as a scene was about to be shot a second time.

If we didn't laugh the first time, then we had to laugh double the next time. I couldn't figure out why a particular scene had to be shot twice, as everything seemed to look perfect to me. It might have been the director wanting a different camera angle, or perhaps a line was said incorrectly. Sometimes a scene has to be shot twice or even three times in order for a director to cut the show a certain way.

Getting back to the episode …

Lucy took Patricia home while Kim waited for Donny to come out from backstage. Kim wanted to get an autograph album signed for Patricia. Donny thought Kim actually *was* Patricia, and fell for her after reading Patricia's fan letter to him.

Lucy actually had very little to do in the episode. She was in almost every scene, but the show focused on Lucie and Donny. I think it was because of Lucy's leg injury; she was just not at her usual speed yet. In the very last scene, Donny sang a duet with Kim called "I'll Never Fall in Love Again," which was a very special treat for the audience.

After the show was over, Lucy thanked her cast and crew and then graciously thanked the audience.

When Peggy and I left the soundstage, the entire audience boarded the Universal trams. We thought we were headed back to Guest Relations, but instead, we were all given a back-lot tour. This was another treat for me, since I usually only got to go on the Universal Studios tour when we had family visiting from out of state.

In those days, the Universal tour included Western Streets, where a lot of the old Westerns were filmed. There was a burning house, as well as the house from the movie *Psycho*. We also saw the outside of the homes of such TV shows as *Leave It to Beaver*, *The Munsters*, and *Marcus Welby, M.D.*

Also, while riding on the tram, we were able to "part the Red Sea," just like the scene in the movie *The Ten Commandments*.

But the highlight for me was when we got to visit a celebrity dressing room. It turned out to be the dressing room of—who else?—Lucille Ball!

I learned years later that it was really not her dressing room but a replica of her dressing room, or the dressing room you would *think* would be her dressing room. It was the size of a house.

We were all able to walk through the room, and we saw many pictures of Lucy, Gary, Lucie, and Desi Jr. on the tables and the yellow and white walls. Also on the walls were large winter-style paintings. There was a nice-sized room just for her clothes and costumes. There was also a room for hair and makeup that had a beauty salon chair with a large hair dryer attached to it. Another room had a kitchen with a dining table. This was most definitely a star's dressing room!

After the back-lot tour ended, Peggy drove me back home.

I thanked Peggy a thousand times for giving me the opportunity to see Lucy again, and as I walked back inside my home, I hoped that my next visit to Stage Twenty-Four would be soon.

Lucy's dressing room on the Universal Studios back lot

CHAPTER 3

Thursday, July 12, 1973— that's a day I will remember for the rest of my life.

On that day, I was picked up from summer school by my parents. My dad drove us to Universal Studios, dropping me and my mom off at the Guest Relations area at the top of the hill. For the third time, I was going to see a taping of *Here's Lucy*. I only had two tickets, so it was decided that my mom would accompany me. My dad was to come pick us up afterward.

I had finally reached the minimum age of twelve and was no longer nervous about not making it in to see the show. I proudly made my way into Guest Relations, carrying my three-ring scrapbook of Lucy pictures that I had been collecting over the last few years. These were pictures from celebrity magazines, TV guides, and newspapers. Countless hours had been put toward nurturing my collection, and I was hoping for the opportunity to show it to Lucy.

After we checked in, my mom bought a hot dog and a bag of chips for me from the food stand, and then we walked over to the gift shop. A postcard of Lucy from the film *Yours, Mine, and Ours* caught my eye, and my mom got it for me.

Then we were called to the shuttle and whisked away on the five-minute ride to Stage Twenty-Four. This time we went right in, as we were the last group of folks to be seated. I hadn't been sitting in my seat for more than a minute when I noticed that Lucy's mom, DeDe, was already in her seat. Without even thinking about it, I got up, my homemade scrapbook in my arms, and went right to her.

When DeDe saw me, a smile filled her face.

"Do you want to see my scrapbook of pictures of Lucy?" I asked her, holding the book in front of her.

DeDe could not have been nicer. She took the time to look at every single picture. She even showed the book to her friends who were sitting in her section. I stood there, giddy beyond belief, pleased that DeDe was giving me the time of day.

Remembering the postcard that my mom had bought me earlier, I pulled it out and presented it to DeDe. "Would you sign this?"

DeDe immediately obliged, writing the words, "To Michael ... Best wishes ... just Lucy's mom."

She then asked who I was with and where I was sitting. Gesturing to DeDe's right, I told her I was with my mom.

"Do you and your mom want to sit up here with me?" DeDe asked casually, not realizing just how much her question would mean to me.

Light flooded into my eyes, and I nodded profusely. DeDe was seated in a section that was dead center in the first two rows. The best seats in the house.

Breathless, I raced over to my mom and informed her that we were moving to DeDe's section.

My mom looked back at me, a puzzled expression on her face. "But the ushers seated us here."

I sighed and leaned in closer to my mom. "But Lucy's mom said we can sit with her."

Realizing the opportunity at hand, my mom's eyes widened, and she nodded in understanding.

"Okay," she said, and she followed me over to DeDe's section.

We took our seats right behind DeDe as she continued to look through my entire scrapbook. I could tell that she was impressed by all the images I had collected. Every now and then, she stopped to comment on how much she liked this photo or that. She liked the candid photos of Lucy the best, especially the ones where Lucy was entering a party or premiere.

After DeDe and her friends had looked through the entire scrapbook, she turned to me and asked me a question that just about caused my heart to stop beating ...

"How would you like to meet Lucy after the show?"

The entire studio seemed to spin around me, and I grew light-headed in an instant.

Meet Lucy? Was she serious?

This was something that in my wildest dreams I had never envisioned happening.

I opened my mouth to respond but could not find words appropriate to match all the excitement that was bubbling up inside of me.

For the first time in my life, I was absolutely speechless.

My mom gave me a little nudge, prompting me to answer.

"Yes!" I managed to finally spit out.

DeDe smiled. It was a done deal.

I was going to meet Lucille Ball after the taping.

The show soon began, and I sat in my seat, trying to contain myself. I tried to stay focused, calm, and collected. It was quite a challenge, knowing that I would be meeting Lucy in just a couple of short hours.

Gary Morton did his usual warm-up and then, eyes darting around the audience, asked if anyone had ever been to a filming of a Lucy show before.

Lucie Arnaz, who was sitting in the audience, raised her hand straight up into the air, and a rush of laughter erupted from the audience. It turned out that she wasn't in the episode for that week and had just come to watch the filming.

Gary asked Lucie to come down and answer a few questions. She happily slid under the railing that separated us from the stage area, walked over to Gary, and took a few questions from the audience.

After a couple of minutes, it was time for Gary to introduce Lucy. This time Lucy came out from center stage, running from side to side at a fairly fast pace, her cheeks full of color and glow. I was happy to see that her leg was just about healed.

Of course, one of the first things Lucy did was introduce her mom to the entire studio audience. As everyone clapped, it looked as if DeDe was trying to inform Lucy of my presence and let her know that she had a huge fan in the audience. Hopeful, I looked over at Lucy, expecting her to notice, but with all the clapping, Lucy and Gary did not seem to hear her.

Lucy proceeded to take a few questions from the audience. A woman asked if she could get Lucy's autograph.

A gentle smile on her face, Lucy shook her head. "I'd like to, but it's against CBS rules. I'm sorry."

That was basically just a nice way of saying, "If I sign for you, I have to sign for everyone."

After all the questions were answered, it was finally time to start the taping. The guest stars of the episode that day were singers Steve Lawrence and Eydie Gorme, who were playing themselves. The show was written by Bob O'Brien and directed by Coby Ruskin.

In that particular episode, Eydie thinks Steve is fooling around with a Las Vegas showgirl. In the first scene, we watched Uncle Harry in the office with Lucy, explaining to his creditors over the phone that "the check is in the mail."

Uncle Harry then turned to Lucy and blurted out, "Carter's Unique Employment Agency better get some new business soon."

It was a very funny scene that ended up getting cut from the original broadcast because the show ran too long. The scene was shot again for the Eddie Albert episode a couple of months later.

In the second scene, Lucy sat alone at her desk at the Carter's Unique Employment Agency, fiddling with her typewriter and singing the song, "If He Walked into My Life." This was the song that Eydie had sung on her hit record a few years earlier. It was also the song that Lucy would go on to sing the following year in the movie *Mame*.

Later in the scene, Lucy crossed paths with Steve and, with enthusiasm blazing through her nerves, exclaimed, "Who would ever think I would meet my favorite singer's husband?"

After that, Eydie told Lucy that she had left Steve and was now looking for someone to do the cooking, make reservations, take care of her traveling needs, and serve as a valet.

Very much interested in the opportunity, Lucy told Eydie that when things were slow around the office, her boss allowed her to do a little moonlighting. And since things were, in fact, slow at the moment, Lucy offered her services.

The filming was moving along as smooth as anything until about the fifth scene. In this scene, Lucy was also moonlighting as Steve's assistant. Also, she had somehow gotten it into her head that it was her duty to get Steve and Eydie back together. As Lucy Carter had put it, "There are not that many good acts out there."

Lucy was in Steve's hotel room, preparing a sandwich for Steve, when he entered. After walking through, he slammed the door behind him, but it did not catch properly. About ten seconds later, Lucy called out, "Cut!"

Steve exited the stage, and within no time, they were ready to shoot the scene all over again. The second time, Steve managed to get the door closed.

I sighed in relief, eager that things were moving again. I knew that every time they had nailed a scene, it was one step closer to my meeting with Lucy! Knowing that that was ahead of me, there was no way I could invest all my attention into what was happening onstage.

For the duration of the show, I couldn't control my fidgeting. Couldn't stop biting nails and couldn't stop the kicking of the chair in front of me. It was as if I were on another planet entirely. One in which realities were laced with the whisper of dreams. One in which all that I had hoped for was just mere inches in front of me, there for the taking.

Throughout the filming, my mom kept leaning toward me, kept whispering for me to stop moving around so much. But it was useless. All self-control had gone right out the window the second that DeDe had said those words that I never imagined I would hear.

When it came time for the very last scene, my heart started to race. This was it. One more scene to go.

The last scene was a glorious reunion for Steve and Eydie, all thanks to Lucy, of course.

When they finished shooting, I sat up straight in my chair, ready to finally go backstage. Unfortunately, the director had other plans. Although the scene came out perfectly, he wanted to shoot it one more time.

Disappointment rounded my shoulders, and I sank back into my seat. They shot the scene again. To me, it looked exactly like the first take, but it could have been from a different camera angle.

After what seemed to be eons, Gary introduced Lucy again, and then she reintroduced the cast. Gale Gordon, Steve Lawrence, and Eydie Gorme all took their bows to an exhilarated audience.

As the performers turned and left the stage, DeDe looked over at me and my mom. "Wait with me 'til everyone leaves."

We sat in our seats as the audience quickly left the bleacher area. I watched as the band and the crew started to pack up and clear the stage.

After about five minutes (or, for me, an eternity), the audience area was cleared out.

Warmth coming from her eyes, DeDe glanced over at me. "Now would be a good time to go backstage and see Lucy."

At that time, my sensitive and generous mom said to me, "Michael, you go, and I'll wait outside."

She knew it would be my only chance to meet Lucy. As this would be a special moment with my idol, my mom thought it was important for me to go on my own. It was years later that I realized just how special my mom was to do that for me.

Before I knew it, DeDe had taken me by my hand, and off I went with her, in the opposite way that the audience had gone. We went stage left, down a small staircase to a backstage area. The first area we passed contained a few long tables and chairs; there was even some snack food still left on the tables. It looked like a place set aside for the cast and crew to relax.

We eventually ended up directly backstage, behind the sets, in an area that I learned was called Lucy Lane. It was a gift from the stage crew to Lucy. Decked out with flashy Lucy stores and boutiques, it looked like a dazzling replica of Main Street USA.

We passed by all kinds of doors—doors that led to the makeup department, to the hair salon, to the wardrobe department.

Then there were the dressing rooms.

DeDe and I walked past Lucie in front of her dressing room, and I did not waste the opportunity.

"Hi," I said to Lucie, smiling.

She smiled back and locked eyes with me. "Hi!"

After we passed Lucie, the moment of truth seemed to slam right into me: Lucy was standing in front of her dressing room, about four stairs up from the floor. I froze, my eyes taking in every detail of the bright and commanding presence of Lucille Ball.

She was still wearing the outfit from the last scene of the show—a navy jacket and skirt, with a white blouse covered in blue polka dots. She looked about twelve feet tall.

Lucy looked at her mom, and her eyes seemed to smile. "Hi, DeDe. Did you enjoy the show tonight?" (To myself, I thought about how strange it was that Lucy was calling her mom by her first name.)

DeDe replied, "Yes, it was very good."

I stood there, eager to be introduced.

DeDe looked at me for a moment and then said to Lucy, "I have a very special person who would like to meet you. He's a very special fan of yours. His name is Mike."

Lucy looked over at me for the first time, taking in my presence. Her blue eyes had a piercing quality that revealed her fearless nature. She took her right hand and gave me a handshake. "Hello, Mike. How old are you?"

I said to her, "Today is my half birthday. I'm twelve and a half."

With that, I held up my scrapbook of pictures, and her eyes curiously studied its cover. I then opened the book up for her to look at. I watched as she looked through the pages, her lips curling upward, her eyes bright with joy.

I had to restrain myself from wanting to dig into my own skin and pinch as hard as I could. There was something very dreamlike about the fact that I was mere inches away from her, that my eyes were privy to watching her every move.

Lucille Ball was looking at the scrapbook that I had labored over for years. That I had put my time into. My sweat, my energy, my heart. It was my tribute to her. It was my manifestation of a creative expression that she had inspired.

"Where do you live?" Lucy asked me, looking up from the scrapbook.

"In Van Nuys."

"Who came here with you?"

"My mom. She's outside. She wanted this to be my special visit with you."

"You must have very special parents."

Given Lucy's open and welcoming nature, I felt comfortable immediately. I moved the conversation along, telling her I had bought a postcard earlier in the day from the Universal Studios gift shop. I let her know that it was from my favorite movie, *Yours, Mine and Ours,* and told her that I had gotten DeDe to sign it.

"It's one of my favorite movies too," Lucy told me.

My ears perked up, eager to drink in the information.

If it's her favorite movie too, I must have good taste.

"Do you want me to sign it?" Lucy asked.

Thrilled at the prospect, I replied, "I sure would … but I thought you could get in trouble with CBS."

Lucy laughed—a carefree, melodious sound spilling from her lips. "I could do it for you."

Lucy was going to break all the rules, just for me.

Before she had time to change her mind, I gave her the pen from my pocket and the postcard. She signed it, "For Mike, Love Lucy." And then she even wrote, "Thank you."

After that, she handed me back my scrapbook.

"You're a very nice young man," Lucy told me, before she leaned over and gave me a kiss on my left cheek.

Then she told me that she had to go back to work, and that it was nice meeting me.

I took a deep breath and told her, "It was really nice meeting you too. I will never forget this."

Lucy then turned away and disappeared into her dressing room with her mom. Then, just like that, I was left all alone. For a moment, I stood there, taking in the enormity of what had just occurred. Then I backed away and went about searching for the exit.

Everybody was gone. I had no clue where to go. Silence greeted me in every direction, in every corner.

Where do I go?

I was desperately lost.

My palms starting to sweat, I quickly walked down Lucy Lane. To my relief, I found a stage door. It led to the outside, right where my mom happened to be standing.

Out of all the doors that I could have probably wandered out of, I chose the right one.

"Lucy kissed me," I blurted out to my mom, bouncing on my heels in excitement. "And check out the autograph she signed for me! Oh, and also, Mom, she looked at my scrapbook, and ..."

My mom started to chuckle as she held her hands up. "Slow down, slow down. You're talking too fast. I can't understand you."

I soon realized that we were both stranded on the lower lot of Universal Studios, with no way of getting back to Guest Relations, where my dad was to pick us up. We walked around the studio lot for a few minutes and ran into a security guard, who called for a van to take us back to Guest Relations.

"I met Lucy!" I told the security guard, wanting everyone to know of my good fortune.

He raised his eyebrows and looked down at me, impressed.

Within a couple of minutes, a van picked us up. During the drive back, I leaned over and told the driver as well that I had met Lucy.

And it didn't stop with him either.

During the car ride home, I eagerly relayed the details of my big Lucy meeting to my dad. And no sooner had he parked the car than I ran out and told our neighbors, Marcia and John. After that, I told my siblings the news, and then put in a call to Peggy. Pretty much anyone who had a capacity for hearing was told my amazing news.

This was the best thing that had ever happened to me.

A few months passed, and on September 24, "Lucy, The Peacemaker" aired, with the first scene missing. The reason for this boggled my mind. It would have continued boggling my mind had I not discovered why the scene was cut during another taping of *Here's Lucy* that I attended the following year.

*My first autograph of Lucy and Lucy's mom, DeDe on
the back of the* Yours, Mine and Ours *postcard*

CHAPTER 4

One morning, I received a very special phone call. It was from Peggy, and she wanted to know if I was interested in attending a filming of *Here's Lucy* on that very day.

Minutes after I hung up with her, Peggy was pulling up to my home in her car to pick me up. And minutes after that, we were pulling up to Universal Studios.

It turned out that, this time, we were both seated in DeDe's section, as DeDe was not at the filming that day. I learned from one of the ushers that she did not attend every show, though she did attend most of them.

Gary strolled out onto the stage and went about his usual routine of engaging and delighting the audience. He told us that Madelyn Davis and Bob Carroll Jr. had written tonight's episode, and had been writing for Lucy since she was on radio performing *My Favorite Husband*.

And then it was time to announce the special guest— the part that I always waited for with bated breath. When you went to a filming of *Here's Lucy*, you never knew who was going to be the guest star—or if they would even have a guest star. So it was always quite a treat to hear Gary reveal a name.

Bringing the microphone up to his lips, Gary told us, "Tonight's guest is a man that you all know. A man who once shared the big screen with Lucy in a movie called *The Fuller Brush Girl*. He has also been a family friend for years. You know him from the wonderful show *Green Acres* as Oliver Wendell Douglas … Mr. Eddie Albert!"

A wave of clapping arose from the audience.

When Lucy was introduced, she came out and kept it short and sweet.

She went up to the mic, welcomed everyone, and called out, "Let's start the show!"

There was something different in the air. I didn't know what it was, but I could sense the energy had changed dynamically from the last times I was there.

Lucy hadn't taken any questions from the audience or engaged in any small talk at the mic. Perhaps it was going to be a difficult show to film—or maybe she wasn't in the best of moods. Someone who had never been to a *Here's Lucy* filming would not have noticed, but I could tell that something was definitely up. Trying to push that feeling aside, I got comfortable in my seat and watched the episode unfold.

In the show, Lucy's charity club was attempting to raise money for underprivileged kids to go to camp. Her girlfriends in the club included Mary Jane and Vanda Barra. Vanda and her husband, Sid Gould, were semi-regulars on *The Lucy Show* and *Here's Lucy*. (Sid was a cousin of Gary's.)

While the ladies were having lunch at Uncle Harry's desk, an idea popped into Lucy's head. "What we need is a big-name entertainer, that sings and dances, at the 'Girl Friday Follies.'"

In her high, super-squeaky voice, Mary Jane asked, "What about Engelbert Humperdinck?" (That was the biggest name she knew!)

Then, a delivery man, played by Jerry Hausner, entered. Jerry was in the original *I Love Lucy* TV series as Jerry the Agent.

The ladies tossed out other big-name celebrities … until Lucy finally thought of Eddie Albert. She figured that procuring his services would be an easy conquest— that all she would have to do is go up to his house, ring the doorbell, and ask him to perform for the "Girl Friday Follies."

Eddie Albert's secretary on the show was played by Doris Singleton. Doris, too, had been on the *I Love Lucy* shows, playing the role of Carolyn Appleby. In interviews, Lucy always talked about how she liked to be surrounded by family and friends. Because of that, she tried to work with them any chance she could. Hence, there were many familiar faces in this episode. It was known that even behind the scenes, there were crew people who had worked with Lucy from the beginning of *I Love Lucy* all the way to *The Lucy Show* and *Here's Lucy*. That was simply the way Lucy liked it. When she formed a true bond with people, allowed them inside of her world, she granted them a great deal of trust, of respect, of love. If there was one thing about Lucy, it was that you could always count on her to be loyal.

And in return, her friends were loyal right back.

It turned out that Eddie Albert agreed to entertain for the "Girl Friday Follies" and also do the finale with Lucy. Oozing with presence and charisma,

Lucy and Eddie danced and sang the song "Making Whoopee." It was quite spectacular to witness the magic in person.

The entire show whizzed by fairly smoothly. They only had to redo the last scene twice, because they wanted to get complete coverage of the dancing and singing. It was sheer pleasure to see that scene again.

Years later, at the Lucy conventions in Burbank, California, Carole Cook (another Lucy regular) informed us that she would dub Lucy's singing in many of the *Here's Lucy* shows. It would allow Lucy the time and the freedom to learn the dancing moves or rehearse other scenes.

I had no idea that it was not Lucy who sang "Making Whoopee" that afternoon. The crystalline quality of the voice, the confidence in the tone, the richness and the depth of the notes—all of it seemed so much like Lucy.

All the things you could do in show business never ceased to amaze me.

CHAPTER 5

January 10, 1974— that was the last time I would be sitting in the audience of a *Here's Lucy* show. We didn't know it then, but Lucy would decide to retire from weekly television after immersing herself in that world for a whole twenty-three years.

My mom called Peggy and said that her father (my grandfather) would be flying in from Winnipeg to attend my bar mitzvah—the big event in the Jewish faith when a boy becomes a man. As it was a special time in my life, my mom wanted to know if Peggy could get tickets to a Lucy filming.

Well, Peggy surprised and thrilled us all by scoring three tickets for us.

My grandfather was also a huge Lucy fan. He spoke very little English, even though he had lived in Winnipeg for some fifty years. He just never seemed to grasp the English language. Yet this did nothing to deter him from enjoying Lucy and all that she was. He would watch her shows with rapt interest, careful not to miss anything. Even though he didn't quite know what words were being spoken, he would always be doubled over with laughter, reeled in completely by Lucy's facial expressions and physical movements. Our deep appreciation of Lucy was one of the things we had in common. Our love of Lucy's galvanizing nature truly connected us.

Since my bar mitzvah was coming up over the weekend, my mom made a deal with me.

"You can miss school on Thursday, but then you have to go back to school on Friday," she told me.

Thursdays were filming days for Lucy shows. Most sitcoms would rehearse all week and then film on Friday. But Lucy and her team could knock out the show in just four days.

I happily agreed to my mom's proposition. *Who was I to argue?* I was going to get to see Lucy again.

This time my sister Maxine joined us for the filming. It was her first time, and I was excited to have her there.

When Gary introduced Lucy, the band started to play the *Here's Lucy* theme, as it always did. However, while Lucy was running across the stage and waving at the audience, the band switched gears and began playing the theme to *Mame*. The movie was to open in a couple of months.

When Lucy took the microphone from Gary, she told the audience about how proud she was of the movie and that we should all go to see it. As if I needed to be told! I planned on being first in line on opening night.

Lucy also went on to tell us that Bea Arthur (who was starring in the TV series *Maude*) would play her bosom buddy, Vera Charles. Also, Robert Preston was to play her beau, Beauregard Jackson Pickett Burnside.

The guest star for the episode (written by Bob O'Brien and directed by Jack Donahue) was Phil Harris. At the time, I had no idea who Phil Harris was and leaned over to my sister to find out if she knew. But she merely shrugged and shook her head.

I found out later that Phil Harris was a successful orchestra leader and singer in the 1940s. A regular on the Jack Benny radio and television show, he also provided the memorable voice of Baloo the Bear in Walt Disney's 1967 *The Jungle Book*.

In the episode we were watching, Lucy was going about the daunting task of getting a band together for Phil Harris. First, she found a piano player, who was portrayed by Marl Young, her bandleader for the last seventeen years. After securing the piano player, she went to work and hired a trumpet player, guitar player, clarinet player, and percussionist. Every single one of them was of a different minority group, including Japanese, Hawaiian and Mexican. Things were running along in a smooth and easy fashion until Phil Harris forgot to hire one minority: a woman.

So of course, Phil hired Lucy—thirty minutes before their big nightclub show was to start. Racing against the clock, he had no choice but to try his best to prepare Lucy for the show.

And what, of all things, did Phil have Lucy do?

He had her clapping to "That's What I Like About the South," which was a tremendous hit of his.

The first scene took place at the Carter's Unique Employment Agency. Gale Gordon stepped out and got into position. I squinted my eyes, studying him very closely. The scene looked very familiar to me.

As it played out, I realized that I was watching the same scene that had been originally shot for the Steve Lawrence and Eydie Gorme episode just six months earlier. It was the scene in which Uncle Harry was trying to tell his creditors that the checks were in the mail. Puzzled, I watched the scene, scanning my brain for a reason they were shooting it again.

After every scene, Gary always popped out, microphone in hand, ready to entertain the studio audience while the next scene was being set up. With his razor-sharp delivery, he would tell more jokes, introduce crew members, and direct his energy toward keeping the audience in an upbeat mood.

When the first scene ended and Gary asked if anyone had any questions, I raised my hand up in the air. He called on me, and I brought my hand down, and opened my mouth …

"Why did they shoot the same scene? I was at one of the shows about six months ago, and I saw the exact same scene."

Gary nodded. "It happens from time to time. If a previous show runs long and we can't include it, then we can add it to a different show."

I still was not satisfied with Gary's answer. With my forehead scrunched up in deep curiosity, I pressed on, intent upon getting to the bottom of all this. "But why did they film it again?"

The almost thirteen-year-old kid that I was, I simply had to know the answer to this question.

A chuckle escaped from Gary's lips. "Those are all very good questions."

With that, Gary tossed a look toward the CBS pages in the audience, motioned toward me, and jokingly exclaimed, "Throw the kid out!"

After getting a laugh from the audience, Gary quenched my curiosity, telling me that they had to shoot the scene again to match the rest of the show. A number of elements could have changed (Lucy's hair, clothing, and so forth).

I nodded in understanding, the gears inside of me turning as I filed the new information I had learned in my mind.

During another break between scenes, I raised my hand again and asked Gary two other questions: "Did you and Lucy receive my invitation to my bar mitzvah? And if so, would you come?"

I had written Lucy a letter, inviting her to my Bar Mitzvah, a couple of months ago. I had sent it directly to Universal Studios c/o Lucille Ball Productions and hadn't heard a response back.

Gary told me no in the nicest of ways, careful not to hurt me. Upon hearing his answer, I wasn't phased at all. I knew they wouldn't come, but I thought it wouldn't hurt to ask.

Now, although I enjoyed the filming that day, it was my least favorite of all the shows I had attended. However, I was grateful, as always, to have been fortunate enough to attend. It definitely beat sitting in class all day.

At one point during the taping, I walked over to DeDe to say hello. I wanted to see if she remembered me. She most certainly did.

"You're so lucky to be able to attend one last time," DeDe told me.

What exactly did she mean by that?

As I wasn't sure how to interpret DeDe's statement, I quickly put it out of my mind.

I soon discovered that *Here's Lucy* was no longer going to be on the air.

The last taped show I saw aired on February 25. It was episode 141 out of 144—one of the last Lucy shows to air in season six.

After Lucy made the announcement that she wouldn't be doing any more weekly shows, I was devastated. It was like the end of an era. Never again would I watch a live taping of *Here's Lucy*. The winding road up to Universal Studios, the tram ride, the thrill of being escorted to my reserved seat, the anticipation of seeing Lucy emerge from backstage for the first time—these were delights that I would no longer have the fortune of experiencing again.

However, as crestfallen as I was, it wasn't really "the end." Lucy had also announced that she would be doing Lucy specials. Knowing that I had the specials to look forward to filled me with a bit of comfort.

But regardless of the specials, Monday nights would never be the same again. There was no denying that fact. Lucy owned Monday night television on CBS for twenty-three years. Her amazing record still stands today.

In Los Angeles, she was seen as many as seven times a day on her TV shows. *I Love Lucy* was on during the mornings and evenings, and *The Lucy Show* played during the afternoons. So there was always an opportunity to see Lucy.

Well ... on the television set, at least.

Odds were that I would never see Lucy in person again.

*   *   *

In early March my dad punished me for bringing home an unimpressive report card. I had never really been punished before, so this was definitely a first for me.

As I was never one who could concentrate and listen in class, it was sometimes a struggle to keep my grades up. My dad, unhappy with the situation, decided that he would put his foot down and dish out a punishment that I would never forget.

And what exactly was that punishment?

I could not watch Lucy for two weeks.

Two whole weeks.

For me it was the equivalent of someone giving up years of smoking just like that— completely cold turkey, no questions asked, don't look back.

It just so happened that the two weeks fell on the time of the last two episodes of the original *Here's Lucy* airings.

During this time, there were no recording devices—no DVD players, no VHS players, no DVRs—so things were looking quite bleak. But there was no way on earth I was going to miss those episodes. Whatever it took, I was determined to watch the last two shows.

Fortunately, it didn't take too much. Although I was serving a two-week sentence, I was still able to visit my neighbors during certain times of the day and night. That meant timing my visits to the time that the show was on!

I think my dad knew exactly what I was doing, but he never said anything. He knew that watching my Lucy meant everything to me. I never missed an episode.

So on March 18, 1974, I walked across the street and watched the last prime-time episode of *Here's Lucy* with my neighbors, Marcia and John. The episode was called "Lucy Fights the System." I invested all of my attention into watching it very carefully, wanting to savor every moment, knowing that this was *it*.

Monday nights have never been quite the same since.

Lucille Ball Productions, Inc.
Universal Studios
100 Universal Plaza, Universal City, California 91608

Cable Address
"LUCIBAL"

January 25, 1974

Michael Stern
13354 Sylvan St.
Van Nuys, California 91401

Dear Michael:

We have just returned from Palm Springs to find your lovely handwritten invitation to your Bar Mitzvah on January 12. Apparently it was mixed in with a batch of fan mail which waited for my attention. Gary and I are sorry to have missed this event which is so important to a young man's life. I am sure your parents are very proud of you. I know we are. I appreciate the fact I have fans like you and look forward to your next visit to my show.

Please give my best wishes to your mother and father and tell them we are sorry to have missed this special occasion.

Love,

Lucy

Lucille Ball
LB:wc

My first letter from Lucy about my Bar Mitzvah

CHAPTER 6

Two of my sister's friends gave me a bar mitzvah present that I was delighted to accept—the opportunity to stand outside the theater to cheer as all the stars entered during the premiere of the movie *Mame*. Although I had never done anything like this before, I thought it would be fun to see Lucy again.

Tuesday, March 26, 1974, was the first time I saw Lucy outside of Universal Studios. My sister's friends picked me up, and we arrived early at the Cinerama Dome Theater in Hollywood.

When we got there, we found that the crew was still setting up all the film gear. We picked out an area that we thought would be a good place to stand in order to see all the stars arrive. At first, we were on the same side as the entrance door to the theater, but in no time, we had lost the spot; we just kept getting pushed farther and farther away.

Finally, we were told by the employees of the theater that everyone would have to move directly across the street. We heard that Sunset Boulevard would close down right before the start of the premiere, so we figured we didn't have to worry about traffic obstructing our view. All of us moved across the street, hopeful that we would still get a good glimpse of all the stars.

But things didn't go exactly as planned. Merv Griffin and his crew arrived and efficiently launched into the taping of their talk show coverage for the event. It was quite a challenge to see any of what was happening across the street. This was because the traffic on Sunset Boulevard hadn't been stopped. Cars, buses, and large trucks of all shapes and sizes kept obstructing our view. Not only that, but horns were honking left and right. It was a frenzied scene.

Yet there was a saving grace; the organizers had set up speakers across the street, so we were able to hear what Merv Griffin was saying to all the stars who were beginning to arrive. The entire cast of *Mame* ended up attending the big event.

I remember Bea Arthur screaming with excitement into the microphone, seeming more like her character as Maude than she was as Vera Charles.

When Lucy drove up, I held my breath in anticipation. She emerged from her limo dressed as Mame. With her black hair she wore a long white fur and a short white dress, Lucy looked nothing short of stunning.

At that point, the traffic on Sunset had come to a complete stop, and all of us fans were able to cross the street and get closer to Lucy. With free-spirited abandon, a marching band played the theme of *Mame*. Pumped up by the music and the presence of larger-than-life celebrities, everyone was cheering and bouncing up and down.

Earlier that day, I had made a large poster that read, "WE LOVE LUCY." Standing there in front of the theater, I proudly waved the sign in the air, showing my support.

It turned out that my sign—along with my arm—made it onto the Merv Griffin show. It was the first time that any part of me had ever been on television. My limb was now famous. I wondered if my family in Canada had seen the show and recognized me from my arm! There was an *I Love Lucy* episode called "Ricky's Life Story," in which Lucy had gotten her elbow into a magazine. It was a very similar scenario.

I watched as Lucy answered a few of Merv's questions and then disappeared into the theater. As I thought to myself how much I would have loved to waltz into that theater and see the film, my sister's friends suggested that we come back the next day and see the movie on opening day.

The next day we returned to the theater, still basking in the afterglow that all the stars had left behind the previous night. I had already learned the lines from the songs, since I had bought the soundtrack and listened to it about a hundred times.

I ended up loving the movie. Seeing it on the big screen was truly an experience. But I was disappointed to see that the reviews of the film were not the best. A lot of the critics commented on how old they thought Lucy looked. I can still remember one particularly cruel local newscaster who said that Lucy looked so old you would have to saw her in half to count how many rings she had.

The movie still broke many box-office records. Lucy fans are mighty loyal.

Even with all the glitz and glamour, all the mystique and romance, all the extravagance and grandeur on display, there was another side to show business. The industry that loves you one day can chew you up and spit you out the next. For in Hollywood, the surface always has to be slick, shiny, and replete with glow. Many critics jump at the chance to spew negative rhetoric, especially when it comes to feeding the flames of our culture's obsession with "pretty young things."

It upset me to read what critics wrote about Lucy's aging. To me, she was just getting warmed up. As far as I was concerned, Lucy was a powerhouse, an unstoppable force to be reckoned with. And as the years passed, her talent and her work ethic seemed to only get stronger; her compassion, deeper; and her light, even brighter than ever.

CHAPTER 7

The day that I befriended Barbara Awerkamp was my twelfth birthday. Barbara was a volunteer at my elementary school, and although she was an older woman, we connected instantly. (Through my lifetime, I've always naturally gravitated toward forming friendships with older women.)

I informed her that it was my birthday, and she told me that it was her birthday as well. Right off the bat, we had something in common. Talking further, we both discovered that we were similar in our love of all things "Hollywood."

Barbara grew up in Hollywood and was once an extra in the Our Gang comedies, as well as the Laurel and Hardy movies. She had an affinity for actor Charlton Heston—the same way that I did for Lucy!

As we grew closer, Barbara started inviting me over for dinner at least once a week. One night she even took me and her daughters, Stephanie and Valerie, on a car ride. We drove over Coldwater Canyon Boulevard, a winding road that stretched from the San Fernando Valley into Beverly Hills—a road that I always got a little queasy on. But my turning stomach was worth it. For Barbara was taking us to 1000 North Roxbury Drive—*Lucille Ball's home.*

When we got there, I peered out of the car window, my eyes wide with fascination. It was the first time I had ever seen Lucy's home. In all my imaginings of it, I had thought she probably lived in a mansion that was comparable to the Clampetts' digs in the *Beverly Hillbillies* TV show.

It turned out that Lucy's home was not a mansion, but nevertheless, it was one of the biggest homes I had ever seen. It was a large house painted white with black trim. There was a walkway from the sidewalk right up to the front door. It would have been so easy for anyone to walk right up and knock. I had always thought that her house would be behind steel gates; isolated from the world in a highly secured area, overflowing with tons of serious-faced security guards. But that wasn't the case.

Barbara stopped the car in front of the house and cut off the engine. We waited, staring out to see if there was anyone walking past the front windows.

There was no movement whatsoever. After a few minutes, Barbara decided to drive around the block to the back alley. The backyard was covered with a brick wall (the same brick wall that was used in the Richard Widmark episode of *I Love Lucy* when Lucy and Ethel were trying to climb into his backyard).

In stalker-like fashion, Barbara whispered, "Let's see what's in her garbage cans."

"No!" I exclaimed. "That's disgusting!"

A few minutes later I was picking through Lucy's trash cans. And after my little rendezvous with Lucy's garbage, I came away with one new piece of knowledge: Celebrity trash looks just likes everyone else's trash. Garbage is garbage, I suppose.

Despite my disappointment, I did manage to pull a couple of souvenirs out of the can—a Marlboro cigarette butt and a wire hanger.

You know what they say: *One person's trash in another person's treasure.*

I don't know what ended up happening to that wire hanger, but years later when I told Lucy that I took part in this small crime, she laughed really hard, telling me that it was actually Gary's cigarette butt in my collection.

I couldn't believe I actually thought that cigarette had belonged to Lucy, that I had ascribed such value to it!

But I suppose that when you dig through other people's garbage, that's what you get—garbage.

CHAPTER 8

With Lucy retired from television, things were simply not the same. The movie *Mame* had its run in the movie theaters and fell out of the spotlight. There was an occasional special or talk show that Lucy appeared in here and there, but for the most part, she wasn't in the public eye. Although there were no opportunities to watch Lucy perform live anymore, my love for her and her blazing talent was unwavering. I continued to watch reruns of her shows and continued to scan magazines for any mention of her.

My rabbi's wife belonged to a charity called Variety Club International. It was a charity that worked to enrich the lives of underprivileged and abused children worldwide.

On July 21, 1975, my rabbi's wife told me that the Variety Club was going to pay tribute to Carol Burnett during a special luncheon at the Beverly Hilton Hotel. And Lucille Ball was going to be one of the guests.

The tickets were $10.50 each, and my neighbors and I bought them right away, before they could sell out.

On that summer day in July, we arrived at the Beverly Hilton early to watch all the celebrities enter the hotel. Buzz and electricity filled the air. I came prepared to get everyone's autograph, bringing a memo pad that I had made in print shop at school. The memo pad had a picture of Lucy from the movie *Mame* on it, along with the words, "Lucille Ball says … There is a memo from Mike Stern."

This was the day that I really launched into starting my autograph collection. The cast from the *Carol Burnett Show* arrived—Tim Conway, Harvey Korman, Vicki Lawrence. Shirley MacLaine was the guest star of the Carol Burnett Show for the week, so she came to the event as well, and a host of other guests followed.

The emcee for the event, Monty Hall, arrived. He was the president of the Variety Club as well as the host of *Let's Make a Deal*.

And then there was Mary Tyler Moore. She hadn't taken more than a couple of steps when an older gentleman asked for her autograph on a photo he had of her. She signed it "MTM."

Looking down at the initials, a shade of anger appeared on the man's face. "Oh, how nice, you signed 'MTM,'" the man spat out sarcastically.

Mary just looked back at him, unfazed, not saying a word. I think she knew he was there only to sell her autographed picture at a later date.

When I asked her to sign an autograph for me, she did so, signing it "Mary Tyler Moore."

When Bernadette Peters arrived, I got her autograph and asked her if she was going to appear on *The $10,000 Pyramid* shows in the near future. Here she was, a huge star … and I was asking her about the Pyramid shows. A few years later, she would become the queen of Broadway with such plays as *Sunday in the Park with George* and *Gypsy*.

Lucy was the last celebrity to arrive. I immediately went right up to her, almost before she had time to even get out of her car. She instinctively leaned back for a moment as she adjusted her eyes on me. I think she thought I was going to accost her.

She looked different. It was the first time I had seen her without full showbiz makeup. I handed her a two-page typed poem that I had written. The poem, of course, was all about her. It went something like "Oh Lucy, Lucy, Lucy—I love Lucy Lucy Lucy." She looked down at it for a brief moment and told me that she would read it later. I'm not quite sure that she remembered who I was at this time, but she seemed to have some vague recollection of my existence. She signed an autograph for me on my Lucy memo pad, writing, "To Mike, With love, Lucy."

When we all took our seats inside the grand ballroom, a scrumptious lunch of chicken, potatoes, and vegetables was served, along with a great ice cream heart-shaped cake for dessert.

Monty Hall introduced all the stars who were sitting on the dais. Each of them told a story about Carol. Lucy told the story of how she first saw Carol on Broadway in a show called *Once upon a Mattress*. Lucy told the crowd about how she went backstage after Carol's performance and said to her, "Kid, if you ever need anything from me, just call."

It was a story that I would hear many times over the years. Either Carol was the one telling it, or it was Lucy. They had a very special friendship, both professionally and personally.

After the two-hour luncheon, I literally ran into Lucy as I was leaving the hotel through a side door. It was the same side door that Lucy used. I swear we must have been the only two people who used it. And it wasn't as if I was following her, although it might have appeared that way.

Lucy was most likely trying to get out of the hotel quickly. After she exited the door, she stood there, waiting for her ride home.

I leaned toward her and asked, "Did you read my poem yet?"

"No," she replied simply, not leaving a whole lot of room for the conversation to continue.

Okay, I admit it, I was a nag ... especially as far as Lucille Ball was concerned! Some things never change, I guess.

Looking back on it, I truly hope that she never took the time to read that poem. It was an atrocious piece of work that I should have never in my right mind handed to her. In the years that followed, I never reminded her of the poem again.

*   *   *

The following year—during the summer of '76—I was in the midst of taking driver's education and on the verge of attending my first semester at Grant High School. Things were changing rapidly for me. I was getting older, and having the ability to get around on my own was becoming more and more necessary.

Since I was a little less than six months away from actually getting my license, I needed to locate some alternative transportation. I found out that I could take a thirty-minute city bus ride all the way to NBC studios in Burbank and watch the television shows that were being taped. (Tickets to television shows are always free and usually available at the studio box office.)

To occupy my summer, I spent a great deal of time watching a countless number of tapings. I watched game shows like *Hollywood Squares, Super Password, Magnificent Marble Machine, High Rollers, Fun Factory*, and *The Gong Show*. I also went to Bob Hope specials and *The Tonight Show Starring Johnny Carson*.

On Friday night, the sitcoms would be taping. On July 16, 1976, I went to the 4:30 p.m. full dress rehearsal of a show called *CPO Sharkey*, starring Don Rickles.

During the dress rehearsal, I was sitting next to a young couple who had an extra ticket to see the 7:00 p.m. show of *Chico and the Man*, which was taping at the next soundstage over. They invited me to come along with them. As it was an extremely popular show and very difficult to get tickets for, I gladly accepted, without hesitation. It had been on the air for the last couple of years and was a huge hit, because of the popularity of its stars, Jack Albertson and Freddie Prinze.

The 7:00 p.m. show was basically the same as the 4:30 p.m. dress rehearsal, with some minor tweaking. I was the last one to be seated for the *Chico and the Man* show. I sat in the very back row of the audience, and the warm-up for the evening, executive producer James Komack, came out to greet everyone.

I remembered James in the role of Uncle Norman in the TV series *Courtship of Eddie's Father*, starring Bill Bixby and Brandon Cruz. With his charm and humor, he set things into energetic motion.

The actors didn't come out to meet the audience beforehand as Lucy would do for the taping of her shows. Instead, we saw the actors for the first time as they appeared in their scenes.

During the breaks, James Komack asked if anyone had any questions, and as always, I had many of them! I was wearing a T-shirt with the Canadian flag on it, and James made a joke about my shirt, I returned with a great comeback and the audience laughed at what I said.

That night I asked lots of questions, and during the course of my interrogation, I started to realize that James and I had a kind of dynamic chemistry. James must have noticed it too because he kept the conversation going with me. Through our bantering, we managed to elicit a great deal of laughter from the audience. I couldn't believe the reaction we were getting. Even Freddie Prinze started to talk to me from the stage.

It was quite a magical night.

At one point, James told me that he wanted me to stick around and talk to him after the show. After the audience left, a woman named Josie Hamilton took me to see James right away.

He looked me directly in the eyes. "Can you come back next week, ask some of those same questions again?"

On my end, there was no need to think about it. My mouth was forming the word yes even before he got the entire question out.

From that point on, my Fridays were spoken for.

The following week, I was on the *Chico and the Man* VIP list. No more waiting in line for me. I now had a special seat in the front row. I had become their "DeDe" overnight. Within a few weeks I was known by the entire crew as their mascot. I would attend the 4:30 p.m. and 7:00 p.m. shows.

That Christmas, James Komack gave me the prop sign that was used on the set, which read, "Ed Brown Garage." It was a gift that I would treasure always. In fact, I still have it hanging in my house. At one time it was autographed by Jack Albertson and Freddie Prinze, but over the years, the signatures have faded away.

When I received that gift, I felt as if I was really a part of something special. It was an inspiring token that symbolized a great time in my life—a time that was shaping me, molding me, weaving me closer into the fabric of a destiny that I did not yet understand the scope of.

CHAPTER 9

James Komack informed me that whenever I wanted to see any of the shows that he was producing, he would put me on his guest list.

And so I went to an early taping of *Snip*, a new NBC series starring comedian David Brenner and actress Leslie Ann Warren. The two played a divorced couple who shared the same house. The show was to be NBC's biggest new hit for the upcoming season.

Snip took place in a barber shop. In one of the episodes, they decided to really push the envelope and introduce what would be the first reccurring gay character on television. However, at the last minute, NBC was so fearful about what the response would be that the show never aired.

I went to just about *all* the *Snip* shows and even occasionally watched *Welcome Back, Kotter*, which James Komack also created. The Kotter show taped at ABC studios in Hollywood, which was difficult for me to get to on my own. I could only attend shows there if someone was willing to drive me.

With the free rein I had at NBC studios, I was able to roam about the lot as I pleased. One day I discovered that Desi Arnaz Sr. was going to be on *The Tonight Show Starring Johnny Carson* to promote his new autobiography, *A Book*. There was no way I could let this golden opportunity pass me by.

On the night of Desi's appearance, I was attending a dress rehearsal of *Snip*. It ended at around 6:30 p.m., and the very second it was finished, I rushed over to the next stage and waited for Desi to exit *The Tonight Show*. In my hands, I clutched a bag full of items that I had brought for Desi to sign. I was loaded with paraphernalia—Desi's new book, my *Lucy and Ricky and Fred and Ethel* book by Bart Andrews, an *I Love Lucy* coloring book, an 8 x

10 photo of Desi and Lucy, and my Lucy memo autograph pad. If I could get him to sign just one of the items, I would be happy.

No sooner had I arrived than Desi was walking down the NBC hallway with another gentleman. The gentleman's name was Johnny Aitchison. He was Desi's assistant for many years. Both Johnny and Desi had their hands full, so I offered to help carry some of the items to their car. Grateful for the help, they accepted. I ended up carrying Desi's suit and shoes, which I considered to be such an honor.

As we walked to their car, I told Desi that I was a huge fan of his. Although he had probably heard it many times, his eyes sparkled with pride. There was such kindness and personability emanating from him.

He looked nothing like the Ricky Ricardo that I remembered seeing on television. He was now all gray and spoke with a very heavy accent, which made it hard for me to understand everything he said. For some reason, his accent seemed stronger to me than when he was on *I Love Lucy.*

As we continued to walk, I told him that I had just done a book report on his new book and had received an A.

"I know all about your life," I told him, which brought a smile to his lips.

I went on to say that I really enjoyed him on *I Love Lucy* and that *The Mothers-in-Law*, on which Desi was a producer, was one of my favorite shows.

When we reached Desi's car, I handed him my bag of items, asking if he wouldn't mind signing a couple of things. With the utmost patience and politeness, Desi went about the business of laying everything out on his car and then signed each and every item for me. At that moment, it was almost as if there was no other place in the world he had to be.

If I'd had six more bags of items, I'm sure he would have signed them too. He didn't rush me away. After a few minutes of speaking to me, he knew I was a huge fan, and he was sincerely grateful for my support.

After I thanked him a million times, he and Johnny drove off. I looked into my bag and could hardly believe how well I had made out.

Desi Arnaz was one of the most gracious men I had ever met. To him, kindness came effortlessly and without strain. Although I never really saw Desi much after that day, I never forgot about that one summer evening in 1976, when he welcomed the company of a young stranger with such openness and warmth.

CHAPTER 10

The majority of the *Chico* shows were directed by Jack Donahue, who had also directed many episodes of *The Lucy Show* and *Here's Lucy*. He even directed a few of the Lucille Ball specials. It was always a pleasure to see him at work. Armed with a great deal of experience in television, Jack's presence made for airtight efficiency during the filming.

Between the *Chico and the Man* tapings, the cast would have a catered meal on an empty soundstage. And I was always invited to join them. At 7:00 p.m. *The Tonight Show* would finish taping, and I would wait for the celebrities to exit so that I could get their autographs.

I was fortunate enough to acquire the autographs of Bill Cosby, Shelley Winters, and jockey Willie Shoemaker, just to name a few. Backstage, I often spent time with a guy who was about my age. His name was Byron Allen, and he was an up-and-coming comedian. I had heard he was one of the youngest to perform at the comedy clubs in Los Angeles. All the comedians knew who he was. His mother, Carolyn Folks, worked at NBC in the Guest Relations department, which meant Byron had free rein.

One night a guard saw me backstage and thought I was loitering. He told me that he was going to call the police and have me arrested for trespassing.

Surprised by the guard's aggressive tone, I froze. Fear sitting like a two-ton weight in my stomach, I opened my mouth and told him, "I'm the mascot for the *Chico* show. I'm on the VIP list."

"I don't care who you are. I'm calling the police," he replied, his brow furrowed and his posture stiff. The guard grabbed me and started escorting me out to the parking lot. At that moment, I panicked and started to hyperventilate—something I had never done before. I didn't know what to do. My skin started to perspire, and my face felt as if it was on fire. I was so terrified that the guard was confronting me in such a harsh manner.

At that point, the guard just stood there, staring at me. This was not the kind of reaction he was expecting at all. He didn't know what to do with me.

Luckily, Bryon was nearby and had seen what happened. He left and came back with his mother, who took my hand and calmed me down.

Shooting an angry look at the guard, she said, "Yes, he actually does belong with the show."

The guard, now obviously feeling regret over how he had handled the situation, murmured to himself, "Yeah, that's what the kid said."

After about twenty minutes, I found my center again. Carolyn took me back to the *Chico and the Man* set.

By this point, everybody on the crew had already heard about what had happened to me. Jack Donahue refused to start the show until I was back in my seat. It felt so wonderful to have everyone's support.

After that, whenever I ran into Carolyn, I never neglected to tell her, "You're the one who saved my life." She is someone I will never forget.

I never did tell my parents about what happened to me that night. I was afraid that they would not have allowed me to return to the studio.

But from that point on, I didn't have anything to worry about. Security never bothered me again.

CHAPTER 11

On Friday, November 12, 1976, I decided to do something a little different ...

I attended the 4:30 p.m. dress rehearsal of *Chico and the Man*, and immediately after that, I went to the filming of a new NBC comedy variety show called *Van Dyke and Company*, starring Dick Van Dyke. As they all knew who I was, the NBC pages made sure that I got in to see the show. I absolutely had to be there.

Why?

Because Lucy was going to be there.

A week earlier, I had been tipped off that Lucy was going to be the guest star. Once I discovered that, there was no stopping me. I simply had to attend. Making sure that I was prepared, I brought a few Lucy-related items, hoping that she would sign them.

When I entered the studio, I took a seat that was off to the side, and it just so happened to be right behind DeDe! We were both happy to see one another.

To set the show in motion, the warm-up comedian faced the audience with a big, toothy grin and asked, "Does anyone have any jokes to tell? I'll give you a silver dollar coin, if it's any good."

Without hesitation, my hand shot up into the air.

The comedian nodded in my direction. "Come down to the stage."

I flew out of my seat and within mere seconds was standing right next to him, the glare of the studio lights in my eyes.

He started out by asking me a few questions— what my name was, how old I was, if I was married. After answering his questions, I told him that I was a huge Lucille Ball fan. Wanting to impress the room, I told everyone that I had actually met Lucy before.

And then it was time for my big joke.

I racked my brain and decided to tell a joke that I had made up, from way back in the third grade: "How was God born?"

The comedian dramatically raised his eyebrows at me. "I don't know, Michael. How was God born?"

"By his godparents."

After I was through telling it, the audience chuckled, and the warm-up comedian looked at me, impressed. He handed me my silver dollar.

And before anything else could be said, Lucy surprised all of us by stepping out onto the stage. Her face glowing, she walked right up to me and the warm-up comedian. She gave me a look and the first thing out of her mouth was, "I saw you on TV."

Stunned, my lips curled up into a smile. "No!"

"Yes!" Lucy retorted, craning her neck forward, as if daring me somehow.

"No!" I quickly shot back, not wanting to lose the momentum of whatever was happening between us.

And again, Lucy came back with a declarative, "Yes!"

The audience howled with laughter— laughter that was much louder and fuller than the laughter from my "God" joke.

I couldn't believe it.

What magical door had I wandered through to actually be standing up there? Lucille Ball and I were making an audience laugh. Together. All of a sudden, I felt magnificently high.

Lucy informed me that she had seen me talking on television about what a big Lucy fan I was. Weeks ago I had written letters to all the local television stations about my large Lucy collection. Days after I mailed the letters, a TV reporter from the local NBC station called me. His name was Ray Duncan, and he wanted to do a human interest story on me and my collection. And that was how Lucy had seen me on television, right from the monitor in her dressing room.

I told her that I had brought a picture, along with a few other items, for her to sign.

Lucy nodded. "After the show, you can come backstage with me to my dressing room, and I'll sign them."

Just the response I was looking for.

After the show, I followed DeDe and about half a dozen of Lucy's friends (including a lady named Thelma Orloff, who had known Lucy since they were Goldwyn Girls together), who were all escorted to her dressing room.

I presented Lucy with a shopping bag full of items, hoping that she would sign every single one of them. The first item I pulled out was a beautiful 11 x 14 picture of her that my friend Barbara had given me the past Christmas.

Lucy looked at the picture and then her eyes found their way over to me. "Do you know when this picture was taken?" she asked, trying to test me.

Thinking fast, I replied, "On a Tuesday?"

The laughter that comes so easily to Lucy came bursting out of her. "No! From what film?"

This was an easy one.

"From *The Long, Long Trailer*," I responded without even thinking about it.

"That's right!" she exclaimed, exhaling with delight.

"Can you sign it 'Lucille Ball'?"

The couple of autographs I had collected from her in the past were all signed "Love, Lucy." The world knew her as Lucy.

But today I wanted something different. At the time I didn't know it, but ever since the beginning of her *I Love Lucy* days, she had been signing "Love, Lucy."

Before Lucy herself could answer, her friend Thelma spoke up quickly and said, "Lucy doesn't sign 'Lucille Ball.'"

And just as Thelma got the words out, Lucy said, "For Michael, I will."

To that, Thelma had no reply.

Lucy was all about doing what she wanted to do. I think that whenever someone told her not to do something, she would just go ahead and do it. Her strong personality simply could not be tamed. *That was why you loved Lucy.*

It was the only time that she ever signed "Lucille Ball" for me. Years later, when I should have known better, I asked her to sign "Lucille Ball" on a photo for me, and she snapped at me, saying "You know I don't sign 'Lucille Ball!'"

Yikes! Needless to say, I never asked her to sign that way again!

Back to her dressing room …

Lucy also signed an *I Love Lucy* coloring book, the new *Lucy and Ricky and Fred and Ethel* book by Bart Andrews, and the 8 x 10 *I Love Lucy* picture that Desi had signed a few months earlier.

While she packed up to leave her dressing room, she signed her script from *Van Dyke and Company* and handed it to me. I could not have been more happy to receive it. It was like the cherry on top of an already amazing day.

While we were walking down the hallways of NBC to get to Lucy's car, Dick Van Dyke came around the corner and thanked Lucy for a wonderful week.

In her thoughtful way, Lucy then asked Dick, "Would you sign the script for Michael?"

At that moment, I hadn't even been thinking about asking for Dick's autograph, and I was grateful that Lucy brought it to his attention. He happily signed the script for me.

When I returned home that night, I felt as if I was bouncing off the walls. As I took my items out of my shopping back and added them to my ever-growing Lucy collection, I reflected on just how fortunate a young man I was.

CHAPTER 12

The year was 1977.

I had already been a part of the *Chico* team for several months. During that time, Freddie Prinze became a hero of mine. With his open nature, he made me laugh often. Onstage, he treated me with such kindness, and sometimes even introduced me to the audience as the *Chico and the Man* mascot.

Backstage was no different. He was always looking out for me. I was sixteen; he was twenty-one. We were five years apart, but he seemed to be much older than I. A sixteen-year-old and a twenty-one-year-old are in such different places in their lives that the age gap seems humongous. But regardless of the differences between us, we got along quite well.

We sometimes ate dinner together between the two shows, chatting and laughing over steaming plates of food.

Once, I told him that I was going to be in Las Vegas with my folks during the week he was going to perform at Caesar's Palace with Shirley MacLaine. He told me that he would get tickets for my family and me to see the show.

Once I got to Las Vegas, I wasn't allowed in. I discovered that you had to be at least twenty-one years old. I could sneak in to see *Here's Lucy,* but—guest list or not—I was unable to see Freddie's show in Vegas. Although I was incredibly disheartened, I brushed it off and enjoyed the rest of my trip with my family.

The next week when I saw Freddie at the studio, I told him what had happened in Vegas. And just like that, Freddie got up on his feet and started doing his routine, just for me. I was an audience of one, and I felt immensely honored. Freddie always had a way of making me feel special.

One time Freddie and his wife, Kathy, showed off their new baby, Freddie

Jr., to everyone in the crew and cast. You could tell from a mile away how proud Freddie was to be a dad. The joy was just oozing out of him.

I got a chance to hold Freddie Jr. for a minute. Everything was smooth at first, until he started to cry. At that point, I decided that that was enough baby holding for me.

Things were going quite well for Freddie. On the outside, he had a beautiful family and an incredible job, a future that was brimming with promise from all directions.

But on the inside, there was another story entirely.

On one occasion, he started yelling at me backstage. This, from out of nowhere. Completely unprompted. He was making a huge scene, raising his voice and making sharp, cutting eye contact. All kinds of words leaped out of his angry mouth. Over and over again, he kept saying that I was spreading rumors that he was on drugs.

What was he talking about?

I had never spread any such rumors. Not to mention that I had never even seen Freddie take any kinds of drugs.

Trying to stand my ground, I kept denying it, kept trying to move out from Freddie's line of attack. But he kept coming at me. Kept the words firing. Kept the eyes glaring.

And then after a few minutes, a blankness fell over his face. It was as if a switch had been flipped off. As if he had been pulled from the clutches of a deep trance.

He looked at me for a moment. Then all of a sudden, there was a smile on his face. "Oh, I was just joking!" he said, pulling me into a bear hug.

Locked in his powerful grip, I held my breath, not knowing how to react.

What had just happened?

Minutes later everything was back to normal, and Freddie went about his business, as if nothing had occurred. I tried to push thoughts of that day from my mind.

And then weeks later, those thoughts found their way into my mind again when I discovered that Freddie had shot himself.

On the morning of Friday, January 28, my sister Maxine came into my bedroom. A serious expression on her face, she told me that she had heard on the radio that Freddie had shot himself.

The news hit me like a ton of bricks. I was devastated. My mind wrapped around itself, trying to find some semblance of meaning from Maxine's words. I truly could not grasp what she had just told me. It didn't seem real. I never knew anyone who would take his own life. It was incomprehensible.

For the next twenty-four hours, I listened to the radio and called NBC over and over again to get updates on his health.

About 3:00 p.m. on Saturday, I called NBC again. And that's when the operator told me the words I didn't want to hear: *Freddie Prinze had died.*

These words truly scrambled up my perception of reality.

He was actually gone.

I simply could not fathom it. I had just seen him a couple of days before.

During the time I knew him, Freddie did not attempt to keep his personal problems secret. He would always put jokes that hinted around his depression into his comedy act.

There was one joke he made about being pulled over by the Los Angeles Police Department. He said that when you see the red lights on the police car in your rearview mirror, it means you're dead.

You're dead.

I really wanted nothing more than to attend his funeral. I phoned James Komack's secretary, Josie, and she told me that Freddie was going to have a private funeral at Forest Lawn Memorial Park in Hollywood, and I was welcome to attend.

As I had never been to a funeral before, my parents thought it would not be wise for me to attend alone. After giving it a great deal of thought, I decided not to go. One of the reasons was that I didn't have a ride out there. It would have taken me two and a half hours on three city buses to get there.

Instead, I ended up going out with my driver's education teacher and the rest of the students for lunch. It was supposed to be a joyous time, as we were all celebrating the fact that we had gotten our driver's licenses.

Although I tried very hard to enjoy myself, my heart was simply not in it. All my friends knew I was very upset about Freddie. They tried their best to comfort me, to let me know that they were there for me. But despite all their consoling words, I could not manage to lift myself from the fog of despair that surrounded me.

I just kept thinking how could someone take his own life? How could a talented young man who had roads of promise stretched out before him take his own life?

That night the top news story was that of Freddie's funeral. Many comedians were present, including his costar, Jack Albertson, and David Brenner, Gabe Kaplan, and Jimmie Walker. Also present were the composer Paul Williams and the singer Tony Orlando, who looked just like Freddie.

Even Lucy showed up for the funeral. It turned out that she was just as captivated by his talent as the rest of the world was.

CHAPTER 13

Sherwood Oaks Experimental College was a small two-room school started by a man named Gary Shusett. Gary met Lucy one day while she was getting her eyes checked at her optometrist's office in Hollywood. He had been tipped off about Lucy being down the street. Like a bolt of lightning, he quickly made his way over there to talk to her about the college he had just started and how he would love for her to teach a class on acting. After Lucy did her homework and looked into his college, she found that it checked out. And just like that, she agreed to do a six-week course. Since she believed that there was no way she could "teach" acting, she agreed to a format in which the class asked questions and she answered them.

The college put an ad in the *Los Angeles Times*, offering Lucy's course for $125. It was to take place one night a week, for six weeks.

As she knew how much I wanted to be there, my friend Barbara paid the entire $125 for me to attend. Her gracious offer touched me immensely. Without her, I would have never had the chance to be a part of that class. After the ad was put out, Lucy's course was sold out within a day. Luckily, I had gotten my ticket in time. *I was in.*

At the young age of sixteen, I was thrilled about taking a course at an actual college. A surge of pride rushed through me as I told my high school teachers about my upcoming Wednesday night class with Lucille Ball. In the days leading up to it, I could hardly contain the excitement that flowed through me.

On my first day of class (May 25, 1977), I decided to leave home as early as possible. I had never been to a college before, and the last thing I wanted to do was get lost.

When I arrived, I was surprised to find that the college was located near the famous intersection of Hollywood and Vine—on the second floor above a Thom McAn shoe store. Definitely not what I had envisioned a college looking like!

The only way to get up to the next floor was by escalator. I decided to ride to the top of the escalator, get off it, and wait there until Lucy arrived. In one hand, I clasped a bouquet of the most fragrant flowers, and in the other, an apple. If anyone knew the path toward becoming a teacher's pet, it was me.

After minutes of waiting, Lucy finally appeared, stepping off the escalator with the confidence of someone who knows her full power. I smiled and handed her the flowers.

"Thank you," Lucy said, stopping to take a sniff of the bouquet.

Then I handed her the apple.

When she saw it, she laughed heartily and said, "I think you're going to pass my course."

Upon hearing the laughter erupt from her lips, my entire face lit up.

For the first time, I had actually managed to get Lucille Ball, one of the most fearless and talented comedians of the century, to laugh. I could hardly believe it. Right off the bat, I just knew that the class was going to be an amazing experience.

The classroom, to the right of the escalator, was filled with about two hundred folding chairs. There was a one-foot platform stage upon which a director's chair stood. This was for Lucy. Next to the chair was a table with a glass and a pitcher of water on top of it.

Upon entering the classroom, I went to find a seat in the front row. After all the students had walked in and taken their seats, Lucy began the course. She started off by talking about how important the class was. She told us how our time with her would have value only if we asked good questions and listened to her answers.

Lucy also admitted to us that she was not in the best of moods. Her dear friend Lela Rogers had died that day. Lela was the mother of Ginger Rogers, and had served as a stage mother for so many young girls in Hollywood. She was the lady to go to if you had any kind of problem.

"I owe most of my career to Lela," Lucy told the class, her voice taking on a low and melancholy tone.

After that, Lucy continued the class, pushing through the sadness and setting all her attention on us.

The experience of listening to her talk at such length was one that I will never forget.

Each week, the class lasted for about two hours, going from 7:00 p.m. to 9:00 p.m. The college videotaped her weekly seminar, and the students were even allowed to audiotape the classes as well. Looking back on it, I'm not sure why I didn't take the opportunity to tape them also. I guess I have always been one to live for today and not for tomorrow.

Each class, Lucy would tell all kinds of wonderful stories about the people she had worked with. As one of the youngest in the class, I was not the best, in terms of knowing Hollywood history at that time. But regardless, I hung on every single one of Lucy's words.

She told us stories about Carole Lombard. (I had no idea who she was at the time.) She even told us stories about how she rode on the back of a motorcycle with Clark Gable. The world she spoke of seemed like centuries ago. All her words were laced with so much allure and mystique. I felt as if I had almost been catapulted back to those times.

On June 1 (the second class), I again waited for Lucy at the top of the escalator. When she was about halfway up, her blue eyes darted skyward and settled on me. In a casual beat, she said, "Hello, Michael."

It was the first time that Lucy had ever called me by my name without me reminding her of what it was. With that new and exciting moment, a page had been turned. It almost seemed as if I had made it to the next level with her. As if I had finally developed a shape, an identity, among all the other people she had met in her life. And considering all the magnificent company she kept, I was quite honored.

During the course, we really got to see Lucy—not as Lucy Ricardo, Carmichael, or Carter. We got to see her as Lucille Ball, the person. There was no stage makeup on her face, just her street makeup. She was real and raw and completely present.

One night my friend Darin, also a big Lucy fan, came to a class with me. Darin was a good friend who I had met in junior high. While talking one day, we both discovered that we had an obsession for all things television-star-related. And we were both crazy about collecting autographs! We became fast friends. While I was very into Lucy, Darin's favorite stars were the Marx Brothers.

On that night at the college, Lucy walked right by Darin, and he had no clue it was her. She looked nothing like the Lucy Ricardo from TV, which was what he was expecting in his head. Yes, she could be funny like her character, but she also had a very serious side to her. She had a no-nonsense attitude, always taking the opportunity to tell it like it is.

In one of the classes, Shirley Hemphill—a working actress/comedian on a popular series called *What's Happening!!*—showed up. She was a large, energetic woman who, via her show, got up in front of the camera quite often. Most of the class would have happily traded places with Shirley since she was the only one who was really out there, working in the "acting biz."

At one point, Shirley turned to Lucy and asked, "How come no one will take me seriously in Hollywood?"

And upon asking that question, Shirley's expression grew very bitter. Hints of sadness started to leak out of her words. She spoke about how difficult Hollywood was. About how she wasn't taken seriously for her versatility and talent. About how she couldn't really find any work at all.

Apparently, Lucy had never seen *What's Happening!!* before and had no clue that Shirley was in a series. But when she did find out, Lucy put her in her place, telling Shirley to just be grateful that she was working.

"There are so many actors who would love to be where you are today," Lucy told her, tightly pressing her lips together.

As the audience consisted of a sea of non-working actors, everybody in the room completely sided with Lucy's point of view. Although her tone might have been firm, Lucy always spoke from a truthful place. That was one thing you could always count on.

As the classes progressed, there was no shortage of fascinating stories. During one class, someone asked if it was true that Lucy had been up for the role of Scarlett O'Hara in *Gone with the Wind*. I was grateful for the question, as Lucy set about telling this wonderful story. She told us about how she drove to MGM Studios in her convertible. It began to rain, and she couldn't get the top up for the life of her. She had no choice but to go into the studio soaking wet.

Lucy was near the fireplace, on her knees, trying desperately to warm up. And at that moment, David Selznick came in. With the dust of the memory dancing in her eyes, Lucy told us about how she had "acted" the whole scene for David on her knees. To give us a true sense of it, she decided that a demonstration was in order. She then got on her knees and re-created the entire scene for us. The class couldn't help but crack up. That was one of the many times she had us in stitches.

But there were also times in which she could really make us cry. Like the time someone asked about Totie Fields. Totie had guest starred on a *Here's Lucy* episode a few years back. I believe the person who asked the question had read somewhere that Totie had made some nasty comments about Lucy during her nightclub act in Las Vegas.

At first, Lucy seemed to not be bothered by the topic. With a shrug of the shoulders, Lucy blew it off, saying, "She's a comedian, and that's what comedians do. It was only a joke. She's a dear friend."

Mere seconds after those words were said, Lucy could not suppress the emotion any longer. Tears started to fall from her eyes and flow down her cheeks.

Honestly, you could have heard a pin drop in the room. We all held our breath and listened for what would come out of Lucille Ball's mouth next.

And finally, through tears, Lucy said, "People don't realize how sick Totie really is."

I looked around me and saw that all the other eyes in the room were beginning to fill up with moisture. Lucy's care for her friend was so palpable, and everyone was utterly moved by it.

A year later, Totie died from complications of diabetes.

*   *   *

By the end of the fifth class, everyone had started repeating the same questions. Judging by Lucy's demeanor, I could tell that she was getting slightly irritated. Random questions like "Do you know this person?" and "Do you know that person?" started being thrown around. Since Lucy was a woman of depth, I was positive that she was really looking for questions that would lead her to those rich and meaningful places. But it seemed that her audience had nowhere else to go.

And so, for our last class, Lucy decided to show *CBS Salutes Lucy—The First 25 Years*, a special that had aired a few months earlier. While the class watched the show, Lucy took me to a nearby room, where we engaged in conversation. As we spoke, I made sure to take a moment to breathe, to really cherish my time with Lucy— to realize how fortunate I was to be in this position. All the admiration I had for Lucy had served as my fuel, leading me to share this very special time with her. And for that, I was immensely grateful.

During our conversation, a few other people walked in and out, including Gary Shusett and a photographer. Lucy asked the photographer if he would take a picture of the two of us. For all these years, as many times as I had seen Lucy, I had never gotten my picture taken with her.

That evening I was wearing a homemade Lucy T-shirt with a picture of her on the front. Lucy covered the picture up by putting her arms around me. The photographer aimed and shot, and that was the last we saw of him. Afterward Lucy, Gary, and I realized that we had no idea who the photographer was. So there was no possible way we would ever know where to get a hold of him for a copy of that photograph. Although I was slightly disappointed, I knew that there would most likely be other opportunities to take photos with Lucy.

It was not until about a dozen years later that a coincidence of mass proportions occurred. I was talking to an old friend Kevin, telling him about my class with Lucy and the picture that had been taken of us by this mysterious photographer.

My friend Kevin said, "My dad's the one who took that picture."

What?

I couldn't believe my luck. A few days later I received the picture.

But back to that night during class …

After the picture was taken, Lucy and I remained in the room. She sat me down, the look on her face quite serious. I wondered what was up. But I didn't have to wonder for too long, because Lucy started speaking.

"Michael, I'm so proud of you. But I'm concerned about your future. You could be my number-one fan, but make sure that you stay in school and get a job."

I knew that I was definitely going to stay in school; but *get a job*? That was different territory entirely. I hadn't devoted much thought to that.

"What would I do?" I asked her, my mind a blank.

Lucy nodded knowingly and narrowed her eyes at me. "It'll come to you, Michael."

My first picture with Lucy (Photo by Kevin Gentry)

CHAPTER 14

It seems that I have always known Wanda Clark.

Wanda, at the time, otherwise known as the "one-man band" of Lucille Ball Productions. You would think that Lucille Ball Productions was staffed with hundreds of people. But that wasn't the case.

After *Here's Lucy*, it was just Wanda and publicist Howard McClay. Answering phones, taking care of any correspondence, making appointments, and accomplishing a number of other tasks—Wanda's job description reached far and wide. She had started to work as Lucy's secretary in 1963 and then soon became a member of the Arnaz-Ball-Morton family.

When Lucie Arnaz married in the early seventies, Wanda was the maid of honor. That was how tight they all were.

I met Lucy's publicist, Howard, who escorted Lucy to all the tapings; naturally, I got to speaking with him. He gave me the number to Lucy's office, and once I had it in my possession, I didn't hesitate to use it.

There was a point at which I was calling the office on an almost daily basis, and Wanda was always there, carving out the time to talk to me, no matter what she might have been in the middle of. With her efficiency and thoroughness, Wanda always saw to it that every task was done in an exceptional way. She handled everything so effortlessly, balanced it all with such sharpness and clarity. I really don't know how she did it.

One day I informed Wanda that I was volunteering for a charity called Children's World, a nonprofit organization that helped children with debilitating diseases. Wanda passed this information along to Lucy. Within a few days, Wanda called me back, telling me that Lucy had some items she wanted to donate to the auction. Wanda told me to come to the Warner Hollywood Studios to pick up the items.

For the first time, I was actually going to step foot into Lucille Ball Productions. Also, it would be the first time I'd be driving myself onto a studio lot.

As I made my way out there, I imagined what would transpire at the studio. Certainly, Lucy would be there, tucked behind her desk, reading scripts or answering her fan mail. I couldn't wait to see her again.

When I arrived at the studio, the guard at the gate asked for my name.

"Michael Stern," I told him, trying to act casual, as if I had driven onto studio lots a billion times before.

After locating my name on a sheet of paper, the guard looked over at me. "You're going to see Lucille Ball."

"Yes."

"Park over there," the guard said, gesturing toward a spot with a sign that read "Lucille Ball Productions" on it.

After sliding into the spot, I made my way to the production office, where I pushed open a screen door and found a woman sitting at a desk. It turned out to be Wanda, a lovely and charming woman, who was dressed quite impeccably. She wore a nice dress and high heels. Later on I learned that Lucy would often give Wanda her wardrobe and let her keep it. Since Lucy played a secretary on television, she had the perfect clothes for Wanda to wear.

Wanda welcomed me into the office with a cordial familiarity, despite the fact that we had never met before. My eyes darted around the small three-room bungalow. I was looking for Lucy, hoping that she might appear at any moment. I soon discovered that the three rooms consisted of an office/reception area for Wanda, an office for Howard, and an office for Gary Morton There appeared to be no office for Lucy herself.

"Why doesn't Lucy have an office here?" I asked Wanda, realizing that my chances of seeing Lucy that day were suddenly nonexistent.

"Lucy rarely comes in to the studio. She works mostly from home," Wanda told me.

On the walls were a few posters from *Yours, Mine and Ours*, *Mame*, and *The Facts of Life*—all films that Lucy had appeared in. These posters seemed to be the only indication that the tiny bungalow had anything to do with Lucille Ball. The place boasted no fancy furnishing or decorations whatsoever. It was nothing like I had imagined it would be. Although I was slightly disappointed, I was thrilled to be in the office, as it allowed me another glimpse into Lucy's world.

Wanda gave me the quick two-minute tour of the bungalow. When we were in Gary's office, the gleam of an Emmy award was the first thing that caught my eye. It was for Best Actress in a Comedy for *The Lucy Show*. Wanda noticed the way I was looking at the award, and she encouraged me to go ahead and touch it. It was the first time I had seen an Emmy up close, let alone touched one!

After our tour, Wanda handed me the auction items for Children's World, including a pair of shoes that she said Lucy wore in the movie *Mame*. She also handed me an autographed 8 x 10 picture and an eight-inch pewter plate that read, "Love, Lucy and Gary." I thanked Wanda for the items and the tour before heading back out to my car.

For years after that, Lucy would clean her closet out for Children's World. Each time, Lucy would give anywhere between twenty and fifty items that were eventually auctioned off for the local charity. I would spend hours with her while she rooted through her belongings and handed off various items to me. Once she was finished, I would then go through everything thoroughly, making two piles—one for the charity and the other for Goodwill. Some items were in such horrible condition that no one would want them. There were items that were so old and tattered that they were covered in moth holes.

Sometimes I would find things that were too valuable to give away. Days later I would show up on Lucy's doorstep with the valuable items in hand, convincing her to hold onto them.

"I don't think you want to really give away your bound script volumes of *I Love Lucy*, do you?"

A flash of light would zip across her eyes, and she would happily take the items back. Lucy was always grateful for the returns.

One year I asked Lucy if she would sign 8 x 10s for the charity. Without even thinking about it, Lucy agreed. We decided that she would personalize each one and that we'd sell them for twenty-five dollars each. Tom Watson advertised this in his *We Love Lucy* magazine. In the end, Lucy raised over five thousand dollars, just by signing all those pictures.

Always one to push the boundaries and never quit, Lucy exclaimed, "Next year, let's try for six thousand dollars!"

With Lucy by my side, I was able to raise more money than anyone else who was collecting funds for the charity. None of them ever imagined that a kid like me could come in and pull off what I pulled off.

One year, to thank us for all our work and dedication, the organization gave me and Lucy a very special award at its annual luncheon. I have to admit, it was quite an honor to be the recipient of an award that was also going to Lucille Ball!

*   *   *

Wanda once told me that not a day went by that Lucy was not asked to be the "Woman of the Year" for some event. I recall one story, in particular, that Wanda told me.

A charity called Lucy's office, informing Wanda that Lucy had been chosen as the Woman of the Year. The charity officials wanted Lucy to attend their event on a certain date. After checking the calendar, Wanda told them that Lucy would be out of town during that time.

The next words out of the charity representative's mouth were "Then do you have Carol Burnett's phone number? We would like to honor her as Woman of the Year instead."

I still cannot believe how upfront charity officials were about their motives! They obviously just wanted a name star to sell tickets to their event. However, on June 1, 1984, Lucy was honored by Night for Sight, an organization that was very dear to her. The Center for the Partially Sighted was paying her this fine honor, and Lucy was happy to accept it. She had a place in her heart for the cause, as macular degeneration had affected her mom, DeDe, before she passed away. Also, Lucy's brother, Fred, had the disease as well, and was almost completely blind toward the end of his life.

With his charm and wit in full bloom, Steve Allen hosted an amazing event. Diahann Carroll (the beautiful actress who starred in the TV series *Julia*, where she played an African American woman in a groundbreaking role that wasn't in the least bit stereotypical) and Sam Harris (the Male Vocalist Champion of *Star Search* in 1983) sang that night, gracing the room with their talent. I was in the audience, along with celebrities like Hal Linden, Sid Caesar, Bea Arthur, and Jayne Meadows. I was fortunate enough to be sitting at the same table as Barry Manilow!

Recently I ran into Sam Harris, and he said to me, "Singing in front of the Queen of Comedy was one of the highlights of my life."

He remembers the night in vivid detail, as if it were just yesterday.

*   *   *

Wanda was an absolute angel in my life. She always made sure that I had tickets to everything that Lucy did. She knew how much it meant to me to see Lucy. Not only that, but I got to rub elbows with other celebrities as well. A couple of times, I got tickets to Dinah Shore's talk show.

Whenever Lucy appeared on Dinah's show, she was quite at ease. Dinah never asked those tough or personal questions. She wasn't controlling or forceful in her interview style; instead, she always gave her guests a platform on which to shine and express the things they wanted to express. Dinah taped her shows at the CBS or KTLA studios, both in Hollywood. When Lucy appeared on a talk show, she was usually there to promote one of her TV specials.

One particular Dinah Shore show was called "Dinah and the First Ladies." It was dedicated to powerful and trendsetting "first ladies" in their respective fields. Lucy, of course, was invited, along with opera singer Beverly Sills, jazz singer Ella Fitzgerald, and Elizabeth Taylor. Elizabeth Taylor was pretaped, so the studio audience did not get to see her in person.

On that day, Gary escorted Lucy to the studio. I went to the studio wearing my homemade Lucy T-shirt. The second Gary laid eyes on it, he loved it. In fact, he loved it so much that he later had me make one for him as well.

Gary was really looking forward to the show that day. He loved jazz music, and the chance to watch Ella sing live was simply one he could not pass up. I had heard of Ella Fitzgerald but had never heard her sing. Jazz was so foreign to me. Since that show, I have been a huge fan of her work. To hear Ella Fitzgerald sing live is to gain access to ever-expanding lushness, depth, and color. With her voice of pure honey, she transported the audience to another place entirely. I am so glad to say that I have borne witness to the live vocal stylings of Ella Fitzgerald. I also loved the fact that she said on the show that she collected autographs as well.

In those days, after the show ended, you were able to wait by the stage door for the stars to exit. There you could get an autograph or picture with them. And so, after the show, I got a chance to collect everyone's autograph.

It's too bad I wasn't taking pictures back then too! How I truly regret that.

*   *   *

Wanda also got me two front row tickets to a taping that I will hold in my memory for as long as I live.

On a summer's day in 1978, Lucy was set to appear on a daily NBC television show called *America Alive!* Jack Linkletter, the son of television icon Art Linkletter, was the host of the program. Lucy was to be the only guest for the entire hour, answering questions from the studio audience.

America Alive! abandoned its usual studio location for UCLA's theater school auditorium, which held about six hundred people. Most of the audience would be from the UCLA television and film classes.

And so, my friend Darin and I arrived about two hours before the 10 a.m. show was to start taping. Before it began, television entertainment reporter David Sheehan prepared the audience, telling us to get some questions ready for Lucy. Once we were called on, we were to stand up straight, talk into the microphone, and sit down.

At 10 a.m., the show went live to the East Coast. Jack Linkletter came out and introduced a five-minute video, which featured a compilation of Lucy's work. Once it was finished, Jack cleared his throat and—with great

With Lucy at the benefit for Night For Sight

enthusiasm—introduced our guest lecturer for the day, Miss Lucille Ball. Lucy emerged, and the crowd hopped onto their feet, roaring in delight. After the standing ovation was finished, Gary Morton was also introduced; his job was to help with the microphone in the studio audience.

They wasted no time getting the show on the road. Questions started firing, left and right. And Lucy answered each one with poise, grace, and an abundance of humor. About forty minutes into the show, I raised my hand, hoping Lucy would notice me.

She did, of course.

She shifted her eyes in my direction, and a light of recognition filled her face. "Yes, Mike?"

And before I could say anything, Lucy addressed the audience, adding, "This is Mike. He's my number-one fan."

Jack Linkletter, wanting a piece of the moment, gazed over at me and said, "You look awfully young to be her number-one fan."

Lucy nodded matter-of-factly. "He just is."

My heart thumping with pride, I asked my question: "Do you bring Lucy home with you?"

Lucy opened her mouth, about to answer the question, when Gary Morton cut in and said, "I'll answer that for you, Lucy."

Gary went on to tell the audience that she didn't bring Lucy home with her, but that she did Lucy-like things at home, like tripping over rugs, and so forth. The audience laughed, elated to hear what things were like for Lucy behind closed doors.

After the show, Darin and I walked Lucy and Gary to their limousine. Once we said good-bye to the dynamic duo, we walked to Westwood Boulevard, a few blocks from UCLA. We went into a department store, where we watched *America Alive!* on about thirty television sets. I got the attention of people who were shopping and told them to stop and watch the television. It was fun to see my face on so many sets at once. Watching myself, I was high as a kite. I was a celebrity in my own mind.

Lucy had actually called me her number-one fan on national television, *for everyone to hear.*

With Desi Arnaz Sr.

With Desi Arnaz Jr.

With Gary Morton

With Lucie Arnaz

With Frank Gorey, Lucy's "major-domo"

With Wanda Clark, Lucy's secretary

Happy thoughts —
Lucille Ball

CHAPTER 15

In the fall of 1977, Lucy was to shoot a CBS special for television called *Lucy Calls the President*. It was pretty much a *Lucy* reunion special with many of her favorite costars—Vivian Vance, Gale Gordon, Mary Jane Croft, and Mary Wickes. The *Lucy* writers Bob Carroll Jr. and Madelyn Pugh Davis were on board, and so was director Marc Daniels.

Wanda had phoned weeks before the taping to let me know that they had set aside a ticket for me. When the morning of the filming arrived, I called Wanda and told her that I was bringing a sheet cake for everyone. The cake was an eye-catching creation. The *I Love Lucy* logo sat right on top, inside a large pink heart. That heart contained the names of all the cast members of the special. Miss Lillian (the mother of then-president Jimmy Carter), who I had heard was also going to be in the show, was included on the cake. But it turned out that she was pretaped and would not be present in front of the audience that night.

I arrived right after lunch. The first thing I did was waltz over to Gary and show him the cake. He then walked me over to Lucy, who was on the set, and I was able to show the cake to the entire cast and crew. They all seemed very pleasantly surprised that a young kid like me thought to bring something they all could enjoy. It was decided that they would save it for the cast and crew dinner.

After that was settled, I was privileged enough to stick around and watch the final rehearsals, not just from the studio bleachers, but from the floor. They did the entire show from start to finish. It was quite strange to watch a show without an audience. When an audience is present, there's an energy in the air. An aliveness. The promise of spontaneity. There's noise and laughter and movement.

But here, no one was laughing. It was all business. All very matter-of-fact and precise and somewhat mechanical.

After a few hours of the rehearsal, Lucy took me by the hand and brought me over to meet Vivian Vance—Ethel Mertz, herself!

"Vivian, this is Michael," Lucy told her. "He's our number-one fan."

Vivian and I greeted each other warmly. Then Lucy informed Vivian that I had a few things for her to autograph. As I was pulling out my items, Lucy told me that she had to go into makeup. And within seconds, she was hurrying off, leaving me alone with Vivian.

We walked over to a camera stand, and I laid out all the items I wanted her to sign. She signed two 8 x 10 pictures from the *I Love Lucy* show—one from the famous chocolate factory scene and another from the episode where Lucy and Ethel sell Aunt Martha's salad dressing (one of my favorite episodes). After that, Vivian also signed my Lucy autograph pad, along with the *Lucy and Ricky and Fred and Ethel* book.

Before I could whip out another few items, Vivian stuck her hand out and moved it from side to side, gesturing that she would not be signing anything else. I guess I had just reached my limit.

After Vivian left me to go to her dressing room, I decided to walk around the stage. I managed to get a hold of the script for the show, so I spent the rest of the evening asking the talented folks around me to sign it. I got an autograph from Ed McMahon, who played Lucy's husband. Lucy, Gale Gordon, Mary Wickes, and comedian/talk show host Steve Allen (guest starring as himself) also gave me their autographs. I didn't get Vivian to sign this time. If I had asked her, she probably would have punched me in the nose. Best to keep my distance!

At about 6:00 p.m., I was told by the CBS pages that it was time to go to my seat. They sat me in the center section, which was reserved for guests in the audience. Gary did the warm-up and introduced the celebrities who were in the audience, including Chuck Woolery (then *Wheel of Fortune* host), his then-wife Jo Ann Pflug, and *I Love Lucy* writer Bob Schiller. I was also just three people away from one of my favorite actresses, Eve Arden. As I had loved her in *The Mothers-in-Law*, I was quite thrilled to get her autograph. She told the audience that she had just finished a role in a new movie called *Grease* and had gotten the opportunity to dance with John Travolta.

Gary went on to introduce the entire cast, except for Lucy, who would make her grand appearance once the show started ...

The first scene involved Gale (who played Lucy's brother-in-law, Omar) and Lucy. It began with Lucy running down the stairs while the phone rang. Then the scene went on, and Gale and Lucy engaged in about two minutes of dialogue. However, things slammed to a halt when Lucy abruptly called out, "Cut." Breaking her attention from the scene, she looked out into the audience, made eye contact with Eve Arden, and said, "Hi, Eve."

Before anyone had a chance to even wonder what was happening, Lucy started to cry. In a small and shaky voice, she said, "You must forgive me. It's the first time that my mom, DeDe, isn't here, and it just hit me."

DeDe had passed away just two months earlier. She had been at just about every taping of every show that Lucy ever did. It made sense that Lucy would deeply miss her presence on that evening. A big part of me believed that DeDe was probably there in spirit.

After Lucy wiped the tears from her face, she began the scene again with the audience cheering her on. With that Lucy strength and gusto, she plowed through the rest of the scene with precision and force.

During the scene breaks, Steve Allen, Ed McMahon, and Gary spoke to the audience, answering any questions that were asked. The entire show took about three hours to film. After the show ended and the audience was dismissed, I got a chance to stick around and watch the pickups, the promos, and the press pictures being taken.

Around 11:00 p.m., when it was all over, I left for home. On my way back, I replayed the happenings of the amazing night in my mind. Seeing all my favorite *Lucy* people was such a thrill for me. Looking back on it, I wish I had thought to bring a camera with me. *When would I learn?*

It was the only time that I would see Vivian Vance in person. She died within two years, after battling breast cancer. Past books about Lucy have reported that Vivian learned she had breast cancer on that very day. If that was the case, she really was a true and determined actress, one who fully embodied that old saying, "The show must go on."

With Keith Thibodeaux (Little Ricky) on the recreated set of
I Love Lucy *at the Lucy-Desi Center in Jamestown, New York*

With Lucy's longtime writers, Bob Carroll
Jr. and Madelyn Pugh Davis

*With Charles Lane (at his 100th birthday party)
who appeared in many "Lucy" shows*

*With Elvia Allman, the Factory Foreman in the
classic* I Love Lucy *episode "Job Switching"*

With Jerry Hausner who played Jerry the agent on I Love Lucy

With Mary Jane Croft, Doris Singleton and Shirley
Mitchell who played Lucy's girlfriends Betty Ramsey,
Carolyn Appleby and Marion Strong on I Love Lucy

*With Mary Wickes who played Madame LeMond
from the "Ballet" episode of* I Love Lucy

With my favorite "waiter" from I Love Lucy*, Maurice Marsac*

*With Roz & Marilyn Borden who played
Teensy & Weensy on I Love Lucy*

With the director of many classic I Love
Lucy *episodes, William Asher*

"Queen of the Gypsies"

From my favorite I Love Lucy *episode "The Million Dollar Idea" signed by Lucy and Vivian Vance*

From one of the most popular I Love Lucy episodes, "Job Switching" signed by Vivian Vance, Elvia Allman and Lucy

Classic pose of Lucy and Desi signed by both

CHAPTER 16

Receiving awards and accolades meant the world to Lucy. In her eyes, they were symbolic of worth, value, prestige. Though she had already won four Emmy Awards over the years, she never grew tired of being honored. And so, when the Friars Club of Beverly Hills invited Lucy to attend a testimonial dinner in her honor, she happily accepted.

An invite from the Friars Club was a true honor indeed. Once a private men's-only club, the organization's roster included celebrity members like Milton Berle, Johnny Carson, Frank Sinatra, Dean Martin, and Sammy Davis Jr. In its thirty years of existence, the club had not honored a single female; Lucy was the first.

Though she and Desi had been honored as a couple with a testimonial dinner in November of 1958, this was something different. This was her time to shine. On this evening, all eyes would be aimed at her. On this evening, she would be roasted by all her close friends and presented with a Lifetime Achievement Award.

There was no way on earth I was missing this event. My only obstacle was figuring out a way to get in.

It was a few days before the event, and I had no choice but to reach out to the prestigious hosts of the upcoming party. Feigning confidence, I picked up the phone and called the main office of the Friars Club.

A lady answered the phone. "Hello? Friars Club."

I cleared my throat and pressed the receiver close to my ear. "Hello there. Uh ... I was calling about the event ... to honor Lucille Ball."

"Yes. How can I help you?"

"Well ... I was wondering if there was any way I could get in? I'm her number-one fan."

"Her number-one fan?"

Great. I had her attention.

"Yes, her number-one fan. She actually gave me that title herself … I know Lucy …" I held my breath, waiting for a response.

There was a slight pause. Then, "Oh. All right. Well, why don't you go ahead and show up? I'll try to get you in," the lady responded.

As I hung up the phone, my mind raced with excitement. I was actually going to the event.

A few days later, I stood in front of a full-length mirror and quickly studied my reflection. I was dressed in my Sunday best. Since I knew it was going to be a fancy event, I went all out that night, wearing a brown plaid shirt and matching corduroy pants. Eager to discover just what the night had in store for me, I hopped onto a bus just blocks from my house. One hour and three bus rides later, I was standing in front of the prestigious Beverly Hills Hilton Hotel.

I marched right over to Will Call to get my ticket, but to my surprise, there was nothing under my name.

I thought maybe there was a mistake. After speaking to several people who worked there, I was able to locate the lady I had spoken to on the phone. I alerted her to the fact that there was no sign of my name anywhere.

The lady looked at me and pursed her lips into an apologetic frown. "I'm sorry. I tried, but I couldn't get you in."

I couldn't believe what I was hearing. *Couldn't get me in?* I had not expected things to go this way at all. The possibility of failure had never even crossed my mind: I figured I was a shoo-in.

Looking back on it, they probably took one look at me and decided against letting me in. I mean, there I was—a sixteen-year-old kid, dressed in a brown plaid shirt of all things. It turned out that the event was black-tie, and I stood out like a sore thumb.

But nothing was going to deter me from getting in. There had to be a way.

Refusing to give up, I hung out near the entrance, racking my brain. While I stood there, I grew dizzy watching celebrities arrive, one after the other. I saw people like Milton Berle, John Wayne, Cary Grant, Henry Fonda, Mary Tyler Moore, Carol Burnett … the list went on and on.

As I watched each of them walk into the hotel, my need to get inside grew more urgent. I stood outside for a bit longer, waiting for the tide to turn, waiting for things to go my way.

And they finally did.

I saw a familiar face—it was Gary Shusett, the owner of Sherwood Oaks Experimental College. He was walking out of the hotel alone. We both noticed one another at the same time.

"Michael! How's it going?" Gary smiled as he extended his hand. His smile grew even wider as he looked down and noticed my outfit.

"It's going okay. I was just trying to see if I could get into the event here," I answered, shaking his hand, hopeful that he might be able to help.

"What's the matter? They won't let you in?"

"Yeah, I guess maybe it's because I'm not really dressed for the occasion."

Gary's eyes seemed to light up. "Well, hey—I'm actually leaving myself. I just popped in to have a chat with John Wayne, see if he was interested to come and teach at the college."

"Yeah?"

"Yeah, so look … here …" Gary immediately started removing his jacket and tie.

"What're you doing?" I asked.

"I'm getting out of here, so you go ahead and take this," Gary responded, smiling at me, holding out his jacket and tie.

I chuckled as I reached for the items. "Thanks, Gary."

"Don't mention it," he replied, swatting the air nonchalantly with his right hand. "You need a ticket too?"

Before I had a chance to reply, Gary was pushing his ticket into my hands.

"You have a good time, kid," Gary said, already in the process of walking away.

Moments later I strolled into the hotel, wearing my brown plaid shirt and corduroy pants, along with my borrowed black tie and jacket.

The place was amazing. There were round tables all across the room, each of them perfectly set and extravagantly decorated. In every direction, there was a recognizable face from film or television—people like Ed McMahon, Mayor Tom Bradley, George Burns, Sammy Davis Jr., Eva Gabor, Gale Gordon, Mary Wickes, and Jack Lemmon. The place was swarming with activity. I took a seat at a table in the back of the room.

Soon everyone was seated, and the program started up. First, a montage of Lucy's career was projected. Next, Milton Berle, the president of the Friars Club, got up and welcomed everyone to the event. With his wit and charm in full force, he wasted no time in engaging the room.

"Ladies and gentleman, here at the Friars Club, we usually roast our honored guest, but tonight we will toast Miss Lucille Ball."

Clapping from the audience.

Then, as only Milton Berle can deliver it, he went on to say, "Tab Hunter likes to hunt … Eddie Fisher likes to fish … and Lucille Ball likes to …"

An eruption of laughter came pouring out of the audience.

After that, it was a clean show. Henry Fonda told a story of how he once dated Lucy, joking that if things had gone forward, the studio might have been called "Henrylu." Carol Burnett also got up and told a story about doing a show on Broadway called *Once upon a Mattress*. She recalled how Lucy came to see the show on the second night and went backstage afterward, speaking to her and affectionately calling her, "kid." Other celebrity friends went up as well, each of them honoring Lucy with their own fond memories of past times.

After the ninety-minute program was over, I went up to the dais where Lucy was still hanging around, posing for pictures and signing autographs. It was the first time all night that I had seen her up close. She looked sensational; her makeup and hair were perfectly done, and she wore a long black dress with black frills around the collar. Her neck and chest area were covered up, which was the way she always liked it.

I greeted her excitedly and went on to tell her the story about how I made it into the event. Upon hearing all of it, she threw her head back and laughed, letting out the biggest roar I had ever heard from her. She looked at my wardrobe, playfully reaching out to touch my tie, my jacket, my plaid shirt. She loved it; she couldn't get over what she was seeing. It was one of the very few times that I really made her laugh.

She motioned for Mary Tyler Moore to come and take a look at my outfit.

"See, look at what one of my fans had to do to get in," Lucy gushed, shaking her head.

Lucy explained to Mary what had happened.

"That sounds exactly like one of your *Lucy* episodes," Mary said, looking me up and down, smiling.

Later on I walked with Lucy toward the front of the hotel, and we crossed paths with Cary Grant. He and Lucy immediately started talking, and when the time was right, I asked Mr. Grant for an autograph.

Though he was trying to be nice about it, he quickly turned me down.

But Lucy wasn't having any of that.

"Cary, you go ahead and sign an autograph for Michael. He's okay. He's my number-one fan," she told him, while gesturing for me to hand out my pen and paper.

Without hesitation, Cary Grant did as he was told. He signed an autograph for me. I guess that even if you are Cary Grant, you still don't argue with Lucy.

Moments later Lucy gave me a big hug and thanked me for coming. Then she was whisked away by all kinds of people who wanted her attention.

I spent the rest of the night wandering around the hotel and asking for autographs. At one point I was in the restroom at the urinal, and when I turned to look at who was next to me, I saw it was none other than John Wayne.

I wanted nothing more than to ask for his autograph, but something told me it wasn't the appropriate time or place. So I turned away and stared straight ahead, trying to act calm as I stood next to one of the biggest movie stars of all time.

At Sherwood Oaks College (Photo by Kevin Gentry)

CHAPTER 17

One of Lucy's favorite charities was Easter Seals. In the *I Love Lucy* episode titled "Lucy Raises Chickens"—where the Mertzes send the Ricardos a letter to apply for a job as chicken handlers—they use an Easter Seals' stamp. They were able to put in a plug on the show, and people rushed out to buy the stamps. Also, for years, Lucy did a bundle of public service announcements promoting Easter Seals.

In 1979 the national telethon was hosted by Michael Landon. Instead of Lucy sending in a taped piece, she decided to attend and do a live plea to get people to send in money. Each television market also had local hosts. This year, the local hosts for Los Angeles were none other than Lucie Arnaz and Desi Arnaz Jr.

A friend of mine pulled some strings so that I could work the telethon and assist Lucie and Desi with absolutely anything they might need. If they needed water or food, I was their guy. I was what you would call a gofer. I would go for this and go for that. While some people would not enjoy this kind of work, I looked at it as a great opportunity.

This was one of my first Hollywood gigs, and I had a blast being with Lucie and Desi over the course of about eighteen hours.

In the beginning, just as the phone lines were opening up, Lucy came by with a few of her gal pals to see her kids at work. They spent a little bit of time together before Lucie and Desi had to dive back into work and continue bringing in money for the telethon.

As Lucy was about to go on television with Michael Landon soon, Lucie instructed me to take her friends to the National side of the studio, which was a larger area where all the action was.

There was still an hour before Lucy had to go on. She wanted to spend that extra time eating and relaxing in a private area before her appearance.

"I'm in the mood for a sandwich," Lucy told me.

Moving with efficiency and speed, I went to the hospitality lounge and found corned beef sandwiches.

My next task?

To find a quiet spot for Lucy to enjoy her food. The green room was way too crowded for her.

I approached the stage manager and asked him, "Is there an extra dressing room for Lucille Ball to eat in?"

Before I could even get the question completely out, he shook his head and replied, "No."

I went back and told this to Lucy, expecting her to be incredibly disappointed.

But she wasn't. Not in the least bit.

Instead, she shrugged her shoulders. "Then I'll find a place on my own. Everyone, follow me."

Lucy was on a mission. In an instant, she was up on her feet, and her friends followed suit. I tagged along as well, delighted by the determination in Lucy's eyes. Soon enough, she found the perfect hiding spot: under the audience bleachers.

"I did this at my shows from time to time," Lucy admitted to all of us. "Nobody would ever think to look for me here."

I retrieved some folding chairs so that we could hide comfortably for about half an hour. Then Lucy decided it was time to go back to the green room and wait to be called onstage. When we got to the room, we found Chevy Chase sitting there, ready to go on camera. Lucy sat right next to him on a sofa.

Upon seeing Lucy, Chevy's face became animated, and he stood up. "Miss Ball. So nice to meet you. I'm Chevy Chase."

I watched Chevy Chase with admiration. It was so nice to see someone actually stand up as a gentleman and shake Lucy's hand. One thing was for sure, Lucy loved gentlemen. Grinning from ear to ear, she was quite pleased to make Chevy's acquaintance.

After Lucy's appearance with Michael Landon, she left the studio, and I went back to being a gofer for Lucie and Desi for the rest of the telethon.

I had seen Lucie at the *Here's Lucy* shows, but this was the first time that I had been able to speak and interact with her. Also, it was the first time I had ever seen or met Desi Jr.

Little did I know that I would be seeing much more of them in the future …

CHAPTER 18

When I met Lucie Arnaz for the first time, it was a very brief encounter that lasted seconds. It occurred when DeDe took me backstage to meet Lucy after that taping in 1973.

Lucie and I quickly exchanged greetings and kept moving. Before that time, I had seen her from the bleachers at the other *Here's Lucy* shows, but this was the first time we had addressed one another. I could never have imagined that we would have a friendship today, almost four decades later.

In all the time that I've known her, I've seen her blazing talent on display in so many plays. Productions like *Whose Life Is It Anyway?*, *My One and Only*, *Wonderful Town*, *Social Security*, and *Dirty Rotten Scoundrels*. Some of them I have even seen two, three, or even *ten* times. Watching Lucie's plays again and again, I learned that no two audiences are ever alike. What can get a laugh one day may not even get a giggle the next. It's a fascinating thing to behold. Not only that, but no two performances are ever alike. There's a refreshing spontaneity in theater that is quite exciting to watch, especially when you're in the grip of a talented and courageous performer. And Lucie was certainly that.

To this day I love watching her perform. She can do it all. She can make you laugh one moment and make you cry the very next. She can sing and dance like nobody's business. There's a fearless quality to her that is galvanizing to witness. *They're Playing Our Song* is one of my favorite plays I have seen Lucie perform in. I am honored to say that I went to the very first performance of that play in 1978.

It was a new musical written by Neil Simon, with music and lyrics by Marvin Hamlisch and Carole Bayer Sager. Robert Klein starred opposite

Lucie in the two-person play. The play opened at the Ahmanson Theatre in Los Angeles for a six-week run before moving to Broadway.

The first performance was a preview, which lasted over three hours. Plays will usually do about a week of previews to get the bugs out before the actual opening night.

After watching the preview, I was sold. I loved the play so much that I marched to the box office to see if I could get a couple of tickets to the opening night performance. The only seats left were in the top balcony, so I quickly scooped them up. A week later, I went back with my friend Darin and saw it again. With all the glitz and glam of the opening night, it was truly a spectacular time. Lucy was there with Gary; they both walked through the theater with their heads held high, demonstrating what proud parents they were. Lucy looked like such a movie star in her flashy fur coat.

When we got to our seats and the lights dimmed, I could just feel all the anticipation in the air. Then the play began, and I watched, transfixed. I noticed that it had changed a lot since the preview. First of all, the unseen ex-boyfriend of Sonia Walsk (played by Lucie) "died" in the preview but actually stayed alive in the opening night version. They also cut out a couple of scenes, making the play about forty-five minutes shorter.

During the intermission, I hung out with Lucy and Gary. That's when I got a chance to witness Lucy keeping her privacy intact, even as two thousand people stared at her. It was amazing to see her accomplish this feat in such a large crowd. She took us off to a corner of the room and positioned herself so that she was facing the wall. From there she was able to shut out the world and have a conversation with her friends, without seeming rude in the least bit.

Slipping out of conversation for a moment, Lucy turned to me and asked me to get a drink for her from the bar. She dug into her purse and gave me a ten-dollar bill. I was only seventeen years old at the time, so I was unsure whether I could pull this off. However, it was for Lucy, and I was determined not to let her down!

With a semi-confident pace, I approached the bar and asked the bartender for Lucy's drink. I held my breath and braced myself, figuring he would ask to see my ID.

But to my surprise, he didn't. He just simply poured the drink and told me how much I owed. And that was it.

Would you believe that the Ahmanson Theater sold me an alcoholic drink?

Walking back to Lucy, drink in hand, I was quite proud of my teenage self.

After the play, we all went backstage to congratulate Lucie. It seemed like about forty of her friends were there, all clamoring with excitement about how amazing she was. The entire backstage was crowded. There wasn't much room to move around, let alone take a breath!

I remember the only star backstage (except for Lucy) was the multitalented Tommy Tune. It appeared that Lucie's costar, Robert Klein, didn't really have any guests come out to see him that night. A lot of Lucie's people took the opportunity to approach Robert and congratulate him too.

The show generated the most terrific reviews. When the play moved to Broadway, it ran for over *one thousand performances*. Robert Klein went on to receive a Tony nomination for his role, although Lucie, unfortunately, did not. That was quite a head-scratcher, as everyone thought she was a shoo-in to get nominated and win. Angela Lansbury ended up winning that year for *Sweeny Todd*. Even though the Tony eluded her, Lucie did receive every other award for the play—and she deserved every single one of them.

When I left the Ahmanson Theater that opening night, I remember Lucy yelling at Darin, "Tell your friend Michael to get a job!"

I merely smiled. Lucy was starting to sound like my mother more and more each day. She had taken up some kind of obsession in encouraging me to look for a job.

I'll never forget that opening night. To this day *They're Playing Our Song* is still one of my favorite plays. I must have seen different productions of it at least ten times. With its brilliant writing, catchy music, and wonderful sets, it is such a delight to watch. The fact that Lucie was in it made the experience even sweeter.

After that, I became a big fan of Lucie and her work, following it religiously.

In 1980, Lucie Arnaz and her husband, Laurence Luckinbill, went on a tour of the country, starring opposite one another in the play *Whose Life Is It Anyway?*, a daring drama that explores both sides of the euthanasia argument with compelling force. In August of that year, the Los Angeles tour came to the Wilshire Theater for a six-week run. The first three weeks had Lucie as the patient and Larry as the doctor, and for the last three weeks, they switched roles.

Opening night was very exciting for me. It was the first and last time I would see Lucy and Desi together. There were other celebrities that night. People like Mike Farrell (*M*A*S*H*), Tony Geary (*General Hospital*), and Neil Diamond, who Lucie had just finished shooting *The Jazz Singer* with. But that night, I only had eyes for that classic pair. After watching them through countless episodes in *I Love Lucy*, it was amazing to actually see them standing side by side in real life. Desi was with his wife, Edie, while Lucy was with Gary.

At the end of the play, we all went backstage, where Desi turned to Lucy and, in a pitch-perfect Ricky Ricardo impersonation, said, "Luuucccy, what are you doin' here?"

Without missing a single beat, Lucy quickly responded Lucy Ricardo style, doing her infamous "Lucy" cry.

I got a picture taken of myself with Desi that night. Once again he graced me with his immeasurable kindness.

Although I am not one to carry around regrets, I do look back on that night and regret not asking Lucy and Desi to pose with me in a picture. As they were no longer husband and wife, I assumed that they would be unwilling to appear in a picture together. In other words, I was too chicken to ask them.

Years later I would ask Lucie, Wanda, and Frank if Lucy and Desi would have posed together, and all three responded with a resounding *yes*.

*　　*　　*

I was a guest in the audience when Lucie hosted *The Late Show* after Joan Rivers was fired. In March of 1981, I had the honor of being at the Academy Awards when she sang "Hooray for Hollywood." And I'm not exaggerating when I say that I've attended her one-woman nightclub act over *fifty times*. I have seen her throughout the country, not just in California.

On one occasion, Lucie was a guest on a talk show called *Mike and Maty*. After her segment, I was supposed to come on and show my Lucy collection. Although Lucie could have left the studio, she decided to stay and watch my segment. I can't tell you how gratifying it was to be announced to the audience and hear Lucie offstage yelling, "Hooray for Michael!"

Now *I* knew what it was like to have a fan!

Lucie's heart knows no boundaries. With not a mean bone in her body, she is kind-hearted, thoughtful, and extremely compassionate. I will never forget when the big 1994 earthquake happened. I had just moved into my new apartment in Northridge at the time. My brother's and sister's homes were completely destroyed. They had to move out of their places for almost a year. I was fortunate, as I got to move back in less than a week.

There was only one problem. The majority of my items had been completely destroyed.

I cared nothing about the fact that my television set or my stereo were in thousands of pieces. Those could always be replaced.

But what couldn't be replaced, I thought, was my Lucy collection, and a great deal of it had been obliterated.

I didn't lose all of the collection, just the breakables. My Lucy dolls all bore a striking resemblance to Marie Antoinette, as their heads had been completely taken off. So many of the Lucy items that I had spent years collecting were gone within a minute. Just like that. I couldn't believe it.

When Lucie found out about what happened, she didn't waste a moment.

She came to the rescue in record speed with her assistant Elisabeth Edwards by her side. They helped to replace everything that they could.

Thanks to her, my collection was once again complete.

There is no denying that Lucie Arnaz is one special person. I think of her as another sister. There is nothing in the world that I would not do for her.

CHAPTER 19

The Mary Tyler Moore Hour was a short-lived variety show that aired for less than a season in 1979. Each week she would have a major guest star. On the day that Lucy was to film, I was sick at home with the flu. That was one of the only times in my life that I did not get to see Lucy when I had the opportunity to. Not a bad track record, but nevertheless, I was utterly disappointed.

Lucy did some publicity for Mary Tyler Moore's show by going on the syndicated Michael Jackson talk-radio show. Not to be confused with the singer/pop icon, Michael Jackson was a British talk show host on the radio in Los Angeles.

I was working a couple of days a week at a local 7-Eleven store. A celebrity kid that lived close to that 7-Eleven would come in and buy a soda from time to time; his name was Kirby Furlong. Kirby had played young Patrick in the movie *Mame*. The day that Lucy went on the Michael Jackson talk show, I was working. But that wasn't going to stop me from listening and calling in. During a break, I called from the back office. However, I couldn't seem to get through. I tried for about ten minutes before finally—

"Hello, the Michael Jackson show," answered an operator.

Yes. My shoulders fell forward as I sighed in relief.

After giving my name and the city where I was calling from, I was put on hold for about thirty minutes. While on hold, I searched my brain for a good question to ask Lucy. I thought it might be a good idea to ask my usual question: "Do you bring Lucy home with you?" I figured that was a sure thing. It had worked once, so it should work again, right?

Finally, I was taken off hold. And within a split second, Michael Jackson's voice was coming through the line, saying, "It's Michael from Van Nuys, California."

I straightened my spine and took a breath. "Hi, Lucy. It's Michael."

On the other end, Lucy's voice came through loud and clear. "Is this my number-one fan?"

"Yes!" I exclaimed, my lips instantly finding their way to a smile.

"Tell everyone your last name!" Lucy instructed me.

"Stern," I replied, satisfying her request.

After that, I told Lucy about how much I had wanted to be at the taping of the *Mary* show, but that I had been really sick with the flu. She said she would be doing other specials that I would most definitely be invited to. I then proudly informed her that I had gotten a new job working at a local movie theater.

She was so proud of me that I could hear her beaming on the other end. "Now you are in show business!" Lucy said in a spirited fashion.

Earlier, when I was on hold, Kirby had come in. I eagerly told him that I was going to talk to Lucy on the radio show. A glint flashed in Kirby's eye, as if an idea of sorts was dawning on him. He left and went to listen to the radio show from home. After my call with Lucy, Kirby actually called into the station as well. Lucy was delighted to hear from him and reminisce about *Mame*.

After Lucy disengaged from the call with Kirby, Michael Jackson cracked a joke, saying, "If anyone out there has never talked to Lucy before, please call in!"

Lucy thought that was just hysterical.

I sailed through the rest of my 7-Eleven shift, happy to have been able to speak to Lucy. Contact with her always had a way of brightening my day.

Lucy and I talking up a storm

CHAPTER 20

In the fall/winter of 1979, Lucy became an assistant professor at Cal State University Northridge (CSUN) in the radio-television-film department for one semester. She devoted her Monday nights to teaching a three-hour class. CSUN was less than a mile away from her Chatsworth ranch that she had shared with Desi in the forties and fifties.

Lucy decided to run the course in a Q&A format. Initially, she thought she would be teaching just twenty-five to thirty kids, but she thought wrong. It turned out to be well over *150 students*.

"I can't teach so many kids at one time," she told me on one occasion, surprised by the large number of bodies that would be in attendance.

When I heard her say these words, I wasn't concerned at all. Lucille Ball could do absolutely anything. Besides, 150 people was nothing compared to all the crowds she had found herself in front of in the past.

As Lucy was putting her time into this class, she wanted it to be a worthwhile experience—to be able to *really* speak to the students, to educate them on all aspects of the industry. She wanted them to know that their approach and attitude were everything.

From her first day with the students, she was out of the gate and running. She communicated with the class in an open manner, letting them know of the rejection they would most definitely endure, fueling them with inspiration to stay motivated.

She told the class how she once got rave reviews on a movie, along with just one sour review. She became very upset with that one negative review and forgot all about the good ones. Recognizing what she was doing, Lucy learned a great deal. She learned the importance of moving on, of not letting the negative get you down, of embracing the positive wholeheartedly.

Some weeks she would show an episode from one of her series, and after watching it, we'd discuss the show in detail and pick it apart. I remember one week when she brought an episode of the *I Love Lucy* show, complete with the original commercials. The class ended up laughing a lot during the zany commercials.

Lucy couldn't understand why the commercials were getting bigger laughs than her show. It really hurt her feelings. She asked the class if her shows just weren't that funny anymore.

I figured that since the class had probably seen the shows in reruns many times before, they weren't geared toward finding them as funny. They already knew what to expect. The students tried to explain why they were so tickled by the commercials. The consensus was that the commercials were just so outdated that they were funny.

Every Monday night, I walked Lucy to her car after class. Her driver, Frank, was always sitting in the vehicle, waiting for her in the parking lot. During one of our walks, I pulled out a book I had found at a Hollywood-type store and asked her to sign it for me. It was called *The Real Story of Lucille Ball*, and it was written by Eleanor Harris.

Lucy's eyes widened when she laid eyes on the book. "I haven't seen this book in twenty years. How much was it?"

"Twenty dollars."

"I will pay you next week."

Lucy had made up her mind that she wanted that book, so I handed it off to her that night. I had no say in the matter! The following week, I received the twenty dollars.

It took me about ten years to get another copy of that book! Since there was no eBay at the time, it was not an easy thing to find. I never did get Lucy to sign a copy of that book for me.

On another Monday night, after walking her to her car, I said, "I'll see you Friday night!"

Nodding, Lucy replied, "Okay, dear."

She got into the car and off she went.

Seconds later, Frank made a U-turn and came back into the lot. Not knowing what was going on, I stepped toward the car.

Lucy rolled down her window and casually asked, "Michael, what's happening Friday night?"

"You're going to a Friars Club salute to Jimmy Stewart at the Beverly Hilton Hotel."

"I am?" Lucy asked, her face washed out by confusion.

"Yes, you are. It's advertised."

"I guess I am then," Lucy shrugged.

With that, she rolled the window back up, and Frank once again set the car in motion.

I suppressed a giggle as I watched them drive away.

My CSUN experience was a great one, further cementing my bond to Lucy. In the end, she had a grand old time teaching a course at such length. She got a kick out of it when students came up to her and called her "Professor." She must have liked it a great deal, because she soon took her professor status on the road, doing one-night Q&A engagements throughout the country.

That Lucy. She never knew how to quit. Her energy and drive would just never allow it.

*   *   *

Friday evening came around. It was the night of the Jimmy Stewart tribute. As there would be dozens of celebrities attending, my friend Darin and I made sure to show up, autograph books in hand, ready to collect.

Lucy soon arrived with Gary on her arm. She got out of the car and started waving to the fans, who were behind some stanchions. Soon enough, she noticed that I was there, and she walked over to give me a big hug.

"Michael, what are you doing over there? Come with us."

I gestured to Darin, who was standing beside me. "I'm with my friend Darin."

"He can come too," Lucy said, gesturing for both of us to follow.

Lucy and Gary escorted us into the green room with all the celebrities and told us we could collect the autographs in there.

What an opportunity.

Blood raced rapidly through my veins as I scanned the room and saw all the familiar faces. Darin and I both got to work, moving through the room with airtight precision, collecting autographs from the likes of June Allyson, Red Buttons, Peter Falk, Frank Capra, Jack Lemmon, Gregory Peck, Don Rickles, Dinah Shore, William Wyler, Jane Wyman, Loretta Young, Henry Fonda, and the guest of honor, Jimmy Stewart.

Darin and I were not dressed for the event, but we were allowed to watch the salute from the TV monitors that were set up in the green room.

It was quite a night, thanks to a little help from Lucy.

Lucy greeting me at the Beverly Hills Hilton Hotel

Presenting "The Queen of Comedy" with a rose

One of the only times that Lucy autographed her full name for me

*Playing backgammon on my birthday. Afterwards,
Lucy gave me the game board*

CHAPTER 21

In June of 1979, Lucy officially left CBS. She had been working with CBS since her radio show, *My Favorite Husband*, in 1948. Thirty-one years later, after new management stepped in, Lucy felt that CBS was no longer using her correctly. So she packed her bags and bid them farewell, moving on to what she hoped would be greener pastures at NBC.

Her first special at her new home was called *Lucy Moves to NBC*. It was a celebrity-filled special, packed with energy and laughs. Filmed at the Goldwyn Studios, soon to be named Warner Hollywood Studios (where *Life with Lucy* would start filming in just a few years), the special had all the charm, wit, zaniness, and humor of a Lucy show.

In it, her character was named Lucille Ball Morton—Lucy playing Lucy. They had decided to use the real names of people from Lucy's life in the special. For instance, Wanda Clark was played by Doris Singleton, who had appeared in *I Love Lucy* as Carolyn Appleby and Choo Choo (Lucy's real maid). Also rounding out the cast were Gale Gordon, Ruta Lee, Jack Klugman, Johnny Carson, Bob Hope, Gene Kelly, Gary Coleman, and Michael Landon; and they all played themselves.

The show was bursting with lively musical and comedy bits. My favorite musical number was a spoof on "Hello Dolly" to "Hello Lucy." The entire special was ninety minutes long. It technically only ran an hour, as there was a thirty-minute pilot built into it. Donald O'Connor and Gloria DeHaven starred in the pilot as owners of a music store.

Lucy invited the whole CSUN class to watch some of the rehearsals. It was quite a treat for many of the students, as they had never been to a studio before. For them, it was a chance to see Professor Lucy in action, to watch the scenes evolve from the first read through to actually taping on the set. The rehearsals and filming went on for a week in November.

Lucy allowed me to be on the floor for all the rehearsals, and of course, I wasted no time collecting autographs.

On one occasion, as I was getting Johnny Carson's autograph, a stage manager came up to me and said, "Hey, you can't do that!"

I froze for a moment, and before I could answer, Lucy's voice bellowed from across the room. "Yes, he can!"

There was one day in which I spent about three hours with Lucy in her trailer. She was playing backgammon with her friend Thelma Orloff.

"Watch and learn," Lucy told me as she devoted razor-sharp attention to the board.

After some time, she told Thelma to step aside so that I could play. I got into position, taking Thelma's spot. A new game started. Lucy walked me through it, instructing me on what to do. Halfway through the game, I noticed that Lucy took a couple of turns in a row. I peered up at her face but couldn't tell if it was an accident, or if she had done it on purpose. Whatever the case was, I wasn't crazy enough to call Lucille Ball a cheater. I kept my mouth shut and continued the game.

Wanda stepped in for a while. She had some papers for Lucy to sign, as well as a stack of pictures for her to autograph. There was even a moment when Gene Kelly came in to tell Lucy that he had arrived for his scene. As all this was occurring, I sat there, thrilled to be getting such a glimpse into the goings-on in Lucy's trailer.

During that day, Lucy also told me that her son, Desi, was in love with Linda Purl, and that she was really happy for him.

"I think this could be it," Lucy whispered, her eyes gleaming. "I think a wedding is in the forecast."

Desi and Linda did go on to marry a couple of months later, in January of 1980. I guess that mothers have a way of knowing these things!

The NBC special aired in early February and repeated again, after a few months, as a one-hour special. (The Donald O'Connor and Gloria DeHaven pilot had been cut out, since it never sold.) The special turned out to be the only NBC show that Lucy would do.

I'm not sure of all the details about what happened, but Lucy confided something to me. She told me that it had been a big mistake to leave her home at CBS.

I, on the other hand, thought it was too early for Lucy to be thinking that way. Things were going quite well for her, and I was positive they would continue in that fashion.

Lucy's protégé, actress Carole Cook

With the one and only Gale Gordon

With the cast of The Lucy Show *at the annual Loving Lucy convention in Burbank, CA with L-R Ralph Hart, Dick Martin, Candy Moore, myself, and Jimmy Garrett*

With Vanda Barra who played Lucy's girlfriend Vanda on Here's Lucy

Lucy and Gale Gordon picture signed by both

CHAPTER 22

As the bond between Lucy and me grew, she started promising to invite me over to her home to visit. Hearing these words was like absolute music to my ears. Finally, I would have the opportunity to walk right up to the front door and knock, swelling with pride at the fact that Lucy herself had actually invited me.

Well, it turned out that the first time I visited Lucy's home was a total accident.

Allan, a friend I had made at camp one summer, came in from San Diego to do some sightseeing in Hollywood, and I offered to accompany him. We blazed through the entire town in one day, stopping at Grauman's Chinese Theatre (where Lucy and Ethel stole John Wayne's footprints from the courtyard), the Hollywood Bowl, the Walk of Fame, the La Brea Tar Pits, and the Farmers Market. And of course, what Hollywood sightseeing trip would be complete without checking out some celebrity homes?

We went out to Beverly Hills, and I parked my car on Roxbury Drive. We hopped out, and I led Allan in front of Lucy's home, launching into the story about how I knew her. I wasn't quite sure whether he believed me. At that time, I wasn't shy about sharing my Lucy stories (I'm still not), and I told them to anyone who would listen. I'm sure most of my friends never really believed that I knew her.

Allan and I must have been outside for all of two minutes when I heard a familiar voice from the top-floor window ...

"Michael, is that you?"

All of my senses perked up as I looked to the window. "Yes!" I replied.

"Come to the side door," Lucy directed.

Just like that?

I gestured for Allan to follow, and we walked over to the side door. Within seconds, Lucy appeared and let us in.

The first time I had ever been welcomed into her home.

Although this was a moment I had been waiting for, this was not what I had envisioned at all. Ready, I was absolutely not. In fact, I looked like a mess. Not only had I neglected to shave that day, but I was also wearing shorts. There was nothing proper about my appearance. I felt tremendously out of place.

But Lucy didn't seem to notice.

After I introduced her to Allan, she gave me a smile and said, "You finally made it in the house."

I grinned back in response, trying to push aside my self-consciousness and enjoy myself.

"What can I get you boys to drink?" Lucy asked.

We both wanted Cokes, so Lucy pulled out these six-ounce Coke cans. They were the smallest soda cans I had ever seen. Later I found out that when you have mixed drinks with soda, the tiny cans are the perfect size.

As we started sipping our soda, Lucy encouraged us to look around the place. It was my first tour of the house. As Lucy led Allan and me through the many rooms, I couldn't help but marvel at the size of the house. It was the largest home I had ever been in.

In every room my eyes fluttered to the walls. I was expecting to see pictures of stars all over the place. But there were hardly any. It wasn't until we made our way outside toward the pool table room that I saw an autographed picture of William Frawley. There was also an autographed picture of Maurice Chevalier, made out to both Lucy and Desi. In Gary's den an autographed picture of Stan Laurel and Oliver Hardy was hanging.

When we got to the actual pool table, I was surprised to find it buried underneath countless items.

I thought to myself, *it looks like my desk at home.*

I thought about how funny it was to be able to make a parallel between Lucy's house and my own. But I knew that it wasn't an exact correlation, as everything on Lucy's table was a treasure of some sort. For instance, a colorful poster on the table caught my eye. It was of "Lucy Goes to Mexico"—a promo piece that advertised a Lucy-Desi comedy hour special.

There was also a workout room in the back of the house. There were *Mame* pictures of Lucy on all the walls. We also got the chance to lay our eyes on her beauty-parlor room, along with the dressing rooms by the pool.

Inside the main house there was a dining room, complete with a humongous dining room table. By the looks of it, I imagined it could probably seat about eighteen people. In the living room were beautiful glass animal statues that Lucy had collected over the years. She told us that Gale Gordon had gotten her started with that collection.

We walked through the kitchen, Gary's office, and the den, where Lucy's backgammon table was located. The den, which she called her lanai room, was where she spent most of her time—watching TV, resting on a sofa, playing games, talking on the phone. The view from the den was of her backyard and the pool.

And then it was on to the bedrooms upstairs. There I saw that there were two bathrooms attached to one bedroom. Both Lucy and Gary had their own bathroom. Gary had just redone Lucy's bathroom, and she was all too proud to show it off to us.

In the entire main house, there was only one celebrity item I remember seeing. It was the American Film Institute award that had been given to Henry Fonda.

"The day after the award ceremony, Henry mailed it to me as a gift," Lucy revealed to us, a proud glow in her eyes.

We went back into her den for about an hour, where we just relaxed and talked about life. The entire time I shot looks over at Allan, who looked as if he could not believe that he was actually in Lucy's home. The bewildered expression on his face was priceless. I kept thinking to myself: *Good thing Allan's here with me; otherwise nobody would believe this really happened!*

After chatting, we moseyed over to her backgammon table, where for a few minutes, she gave me some more tips on how to play the game.

When Allan and I pulled away from Lucy's home, we both quietly reflected on the time we had just had. Lucy's generosity and welcoming openness on that day will be forever etched into my mind.

In the months and years that followed, I made many other visits to Lucy's home. But I knew not to bring any other friends with me. For Lucy was Lucille Morton, and not "Lucille Ball" during those visits. At peace, completely relaxed, raw beyond all else. That she was allowing me into her sacred space indicated her level of comfort with me, and I didn't want to violate that by bringing other guests.

My friendship with Lucy had nothing to do with grandstanding in front of my other friends. I wasn't on the lookout for opportunities to show Lucy off to this person or that person. My time spent in her home was very special to me. It was a chance to spend time with her and see her at her most vulnerable and carefree.

I brought friends to TV tapings and special events where Lucy was going to be the performer, the entertainer, the woman in the spotlight. That was a whole different playing field. I would never have thought of bringing a camera to her house for a photo op. I knew better than that.

One time I brought my camera to a Bob Hope special and snapped pictures of Lucy right before she was to go onstage. Every element about her spelled L-u-c-i-l-l-e B-a-l-l. Looking stunning at twelve feet tall, she was perfectly made-up.

After her segment, she immediately got out of her stage makeup, and a wave of relaxation washed over her. It was almost as if her whole body had melted into the ground, transforming her state into one of mellowness. This was the state that I was most familiar with.

Behind the costume, behind the foundation and lipstick and mascara, resided Lucille Morton, the wife and mother. The most loyal and reliable friend, second to none.

Backstage at the Bob Hope Special before she went on stage

*Backstage at the Bob Hope Special after
she took off her stage make-up*

*　　　*　　　*

The first few times I ever met Frank Gorey was through a peephole. I only knew him from his left eye. To this day I would recognize that eye anywhere. That's not something you can say about everyone you meet!

Whenever Frank would answer the door at Lucy's house, he'd open up the peephole and press his blue eye up against it. It wasn't difficult getting to Lucy's front door at 1000 Roxbury Drive in Beverly Hills. As I mentioned before, there were absolutely no gates between the street and her front door. All you had to do was walk down a long walkway, and voila—you'd have Frank's baby blue looking out at you in no time.

On the stoop was a doormat that had the letter *M* for Morton on it. The single door was large and white, with a knocker on it. Once you knocked, Frank never wasted any time in coming to the door. He would always say hello and was as friendly as the person who was knocking.

Whenever anybody came to the door, the question that was most frequently asked was "Is Lucy home?"

In reply, Frank used one of three answers. "I'm sorry, Lucy's not home," "She is working at the studio," or "She is out of town." He would say this, despite the fact that Lucy was only a few feet away, playing backgammon in the lanai room.

Once Frank knew I was legit, he would let me in, whether I was expected or not. Frank was one of the few true gentlemen left in the world. With the utmost patience and class, he opened doors for ladies. That kind of behavior was like breathing to him. His politeness stretched far and wide, touching everyone he was in contact with. I always thought he should teach a class *on class*.

With him, there was always sophistication. There were always pleasantries exchanged.

How are you doing, sir?

Thank you, sir.

Can I get you anything, sir?

Frank was the kind of gentleman who always had time for you. He could be in the middle of a dozen different tasks, and he would still make time for you. Frank was the one that Lucy went to if she needed a hand with anything.

He started out in 1959, driving Lucy and Desi Sr. around to all their tapings, appointments, and celebrity events. When they separated, Frank stayed with Lucy, driving Lucie and Desi Jr. to and from school until they were old enough to drive themselves. Frank traveled with Lucy and the kids to New York in 1961, where he drove Lucy to and from her play *Wildcat*. He also acted as her security guard, protecting her and making sure she was always taken care of.

One of the first times I met Frank (minus the peephole) was when he was driving DeDe around. The doctors had told her to stop driving. Frank confided to me that he would never get lost while driving Lucy or any of her family around, because he would always do a test run first.

Smart man, that Frank.

Not only did he take the cake as the classiest and most polite driver/security guard I knew, he wrapped a mean package. During the holidays, Lucy's dining room table looked like the Macy's department store gift-wrapping area, with Frank standing over the table meticulously wrapping hundreds of Christmas gifts, one after the other.

What I loved most about Lucy was how loyal she was to those who were loyal to her. Frank stayed on with Lucy for many years, until her death. In an ever-changing world where people come and go, Lucy kept many strong relationships that stood the test of time. I believe that by looking at the way someone handles his or her relationships in life, you can gain a great deal of insight into their character. In that regard, Lucy's character was off-the-charts amazing.

CHAPTER 23

On the day of my nineteenth birthday, I received a surprise call from—who else?—Lucy. It was a Saturday, and the house was full of friends and family, all there to help me celebrate my special day.

In the middle of the party, the phone rang. My brother-in-law Ricky answered it.

"Hello."

"Hi, this is Lucy."

My brother-in-law smirked, not believing it was her. "This is Ricky."

"Hi, Ricky; it's Lucy. I'm looking for Michael."

Ricky quizzically looked at the phone in his hand. After a few seconds, he realized that the voice on the other end was completely sincere. He looked over his shoulder and called out to me, "Michael, Lucy's on the phone."

Now it was my turn to assume the whole thing was a big joke. Never in a million years did I believe that Lucy was going to call me on my birthday. Nevertheless, I took the phone from Ricky and pressed it against my ear. "Hello?"

Lucy's voice came bursting from the other end, and I just about fell over from shock.

"Wanda told me it was your birthday, so I wanted to wish you a happy birthday."

Wow.

"So who's at your party?" Lucy asked, curious.

As I was made utterly speechless by Lucy's thoughtful call, I stumbled through a response, naming a few names.

She told me to expect a present from her on Monday, and we continued talking for about five more minutes. I could've probably gone on longer, but

Lucy ended the conversation, saying, "Michael, I've taken too much of your time away from your party. You should get back to your guests."

On Monday, Frank drove to my house and handed me my birthday present from Lucy. It was a wonderful clock. I couldn't believe that Lucy had actually bought me a gift. To this day, I constantly look at that clock, remembering the pulse of elation I felt when I received it. Lucy knew just how to make a person's birthday truly special.

The following year, I had another special birthday that involved Lucy.

Part restaurant and part backgammon club, Pips International was located in Beverly Hills. Given Lucy's penchant for backgammon, Pips was a place where she spent a great deal of time.

In January of 1981, over the course of three days (the ninth, tenth, and eleventh), Lucy hosted a backgammon tournament. All the proceeds were going to the Orthopedic Ward at the Children's Hospital of Los Angeles. I was especially excited about this event, as it fell on my birthday weekend … and what better way to celebrate than with Lucy and a bunch of stars?

The opening night gala was a hit. Appetizers and beverages were served left and right. The likes of Hal Linden, Dodger great Tommy Lasorda, Lee Majors, Pat Sajak, and Hugh O'Brien were there. Lucy's *Wildcat* costars, Swen Swenson and Paula Stewart, also stopped by to join in on the festivities.

The second day (Saturday) marked the official beginning of the tournament. Earlier, Lucy had made a donation in my name, which gave me privileges to join in on the tournament. Since I wasn't much of a player, I was eliminated during the first round. Lucy had only given me a couple of quick lessons in the past, and I wasn't quite familiar with the game yet. I didn't mind the loss too much, as I was still allowed to stick around all weekend!

For most of Saturday, I helped to sell raffle tickets at five dollars a piece. With the sway and ease of an expert salesman, I managed to sell a great number of tickets. Navigating the crowds and interacting with others came so naturally to me.

I must have found my calling, I thought to myself.

A professional photographer took some great pictures of me and Lucy that day in the lobby of the restaurant, along with pictures of us playing backgammon. During the photo shoot, Lucy couldn't help but keep playing with my hair. She dug her fingers right in, pulling at my strands in fascination.

"Boy, what I could do with this thick hair," she told me, shaking her head from side to side.

(In the past, I had been told by Irma Kusely, Lucy's hairdresser, that Lucy would have loved to have been a hairdresser herself. Somehow, I can't quite picture it.)

I spent most of the final day of the tournament with Lucy, Paula Stewart, and Gary's sister, Helen. Seeing it as the perfect opportunity, I asked Lucy if my parents could come by the club to meet her. Within a minute, she made sure that my parents were on the guest list so that they would have no problems getting in.

Right after lunch, around 2:00 p.m., I saw my parents walking into the club. Lucy and I were sitting at a backgammon table on the other side of the room. I leaned toward her and motioned toward my mom and dad. "Here come my parents."

The features on Lucy's face brightened, and she sprung from her seat, practically running over to my parents. "It's about time we met!" Lucy proclaimed, greeting my folks with kisses on the cheek.

From across the room, I watched as my parents interacted with Lucy, their faces radiant with delight.

Later on my parents told me about how Lucy would not stop gushing about me. She told them that they must have been so proud of their son. Upon hearing this later, I was immensely flattered.

When it came time for the raffle prizes, I helped Lucy with the drawings drum, and we picked out the tickets together. One of the tickets that Lucy pulled out had my name on it. Earlier, Lucy had bought fifty dollars worth of raffle tickets and told me to put my name on them. I ended up winning a convection air oven.

After the event, Lucy thanked me for working so hard. Although I had put in an extraordinary amount of time and energy, it didn't feel like I was "working" in the least bit. There was a certain kind of exhilaration that came from selling so many raffle tickets for a good cause.

The very next day, Lucy called me to thank me again, and to wish me a happy birthday.

"It was wonderful to finally meet your parents," she told me. "You're so lucky to have them."

CHAPTER 24

I figured it was finally time to get a real full-time job—something that paid more than minimum wage. One afternoon I strolled over to the local mall and applied for a job at the May Company. It was a large department store that contained just about everything within its five floors.

Once I filled out my application, I was hired on the spot. They wanted me to start right away. I was to work in the linens department on the third floor. Now at the time, I knew absolutely nothing about linens. But I needed the job, so I took it.

To my surprise, I became a linens salesperson extraordinaire in no time, learning all about the differences between 180- and 200-thread-count sheets, between down pillows and feather pillows, between silks and satins. Within a couple of months, I was outselling the top saleswoman, who had been in the department for years. Though we weren't on commission, those saleswomen were not kidding around when it came to selling.

There was one time when I was helping a female customer locate specific linens only to be abruptly cut off by a shrill voice behind me.

"That's my customer! I helped her last month."

I turned around, and there was Miss Former Top Saleswoman. She shot me an icy glare and motioned for the customer to follow her.

Needless to say, I was not her favorite coworker, nor was I the favorite of the entire sales department, for that matter. I did, however, receive a great deal of appreciation from management, which was absolutely crazy about the amount of linens that I was moving out the door.

Soon after I started working, I phoned Wanda; I wanted her to tell Lucy all about my new job.

Within a few days, Wanda called back, chattering about how proud Lucy was of my newfound employment and how she wanted to come by and visit one day. I hung up the phone and thought nothing of it.

Weeks later, on Memorial Day weekend, I got a phone call from Wanda at work. She told me that Lucy was on her way to the store with her good friend Mary Wickes. Mary was a character actress, who had played a ballet teacher named Madame LeMond in the *I Love Lucy* episode #19: "The Ballet."

Minutes later, I was standing there anxiously watching as Lucy and Mary rode the escalator up toward me. I couldn't help but smile—seeing Lucy at my place of employment was nothing short of surreal.

When Lucy saw me, her eyes lit up. As she stepped firmly off the escalator, she wasted no time in announcing her agenda for the day. "Okay, so ... I'm here to see you work. I want you to help me pick out some linens for the house. That's all I'm here for. I don't want to meet your friends."

Her tone was very matter-of-fact. That was Lucy for you—always straightforward and to the point.

I nodded in understanding. On that day, she simply did not want to be bothered with autographs and introductions. On that day, she was Mrs. Morton, and not the actress Lucille Ball. On that day, she was just another customer, shopping for linens on the third floor of the May Company.

She pulled out her shopping list and went right to work, rooting through linens in search of beiges and whites. She inquired about sales items, and I directed her toward them. She was interested in various sets, and I made my recommendations.

As we shopped, customers stopped to watch. It wasn't every day that a huge star walked into a department store in North Hollywood. There was actually a May Company right down the street from Lucy, right in her posh Beverly Hills neighborhood, where seeing stars was an everyday occurrence. But on that day, Lucy opted to make the twenty-five-minute drive to watch me work. And there she was, much to everyone's amazement.

Though it was obvious that everyone was looking at her, Lucy gave no indication that she was aware of it. She buried her head in the business of linens, speaking to me and Mary as if we were the only people in the store. Nobody approached her for a full forty-five minutes until ...

"Excuse me?"

We turned to see a young girl standing there. She was tightly grasping a pen and piece of paper in her hands. "Can I have your autograph?"

Lucy opened her mouth to answer, but before she could say anything, Mary stepped forward, straining her lips into a smile. "I'm sorry, but she can't sign right now."

But Lucy had other plans. She reached for the young girl's pen and paper. "Well, sure I can."

That was the only autograph she signed all afternoon.

After making that young girl's day, Lucy announced that she was ready to go to the register. Since she had over thirty items, it took some time to ring her up. Back in those days, you had to punch in the numbers (ten digits) for each item, one at a time. When I was finally finished, the total came out to over six hundred dollars. Lucy handed me her department store card, and I ran it through. For some reason, the card was declined. Confusion washed over Lucy's face—she wasn't sure why the card wasn't going through.

I wanted to show Lucy that I could fix the problem, so I immediately called the downtown credit department.

"Hello, how can I help you?" came a woman's voice on the other end of the phone.

"Yes, hi, I'm calling from the May Company. I'm trying to ring up a customer, but for some reason, her card won't go through," I explained.

"Okay, can I have the card number?"

I held up the card and read the number to her.

"Great. And can you check the customer's ID, please?"

I looked up at Lucy, who was chatting with Mary about something. Then I quietly said into the phone, "It's Lucille Ball."

I didn't want to be too loud and welcome any unwanted attention. I knew that Lucy wouldn't be crazy about that.

The lady on the other end sighed. "Would you please ask for her identification?"

"I said, it's Lucille Ball."

But the lady on the phone wasn't having it. "Just—please—ask for her ID."

The lady was trying to remain patient, but I could hear the agitation cutting through her words. She didn't believe me, and she wanted to get the phone call over with.

So I did what I had to do. I asked for Lucy's driver's license.

Lucy gave me a funny look, scrunching her forehead and peering over at me through squinted eyes. "What? You don't know who I am?"

I shrugged and gestured toward the phone.

Lucy reached into her purse and pulled out her driver's license.

"Thanks," I mouthed.

I read her license number to the lady on the other end and waited.

She was silent for a moment; all I could hear was her breathing, mixed with the tapping of keys. Then I heard her breath catch in her throat ...

"Oh my God! It's Lucille Ball!"

I sighed. "Yes, I know."

It turned out that Lucy's card had been declined because she had not used it in years. All she had to do was reactivate it.

And so, Lucy brought her card back to life in a few quick minutes over the phone. But there was yet another inconvenience that she would have to endure; I informed her that I had to re-ring all her items.

Upon hearing this, Lucy frowned. "Well. I'm really running out of time here. I don't think I can wait."

In that moment, the store manager, Mr. Lipton, approached us. He smiled and tried to make eye contact with Lucy. When that didn't work, he looked over at me and nodded slightly, as if waiting to be introduced.

Though Lucy had said that she wanted no introductions, I figured it would be okay to acquaint her with my boss. Once I did so, I explained the present situation to Mr. Lipton, and without hesitation, he gave me special approval to have all the items delivered to Lucy's home that night.

Lucy was delighted to hear it. Beaming, she told Mr. Lipton that he had a great young gentleman working for him. I averted my eyes to the floor and blushed.

Next thing I knew, Lucy was leaning over and kissing me good-bye. "I'm glad you're working. You did such a great job today," she exclaimed rather loudly.

Again, I blushed with embarrassment. Then I quickly scanned the area around me to make sure no one was standing around and watching.

"Thanks, Lucy," I replied.

"Next time you have a day off, call me and we'll play backgammon. How does that sound?"

"That sounds great."

And with that, Lucy and her friend Mary left the store.

Later that evening, after I left work, I drove to Beverly Hills and knocked on Lucy's front door, carrying two large bags.

I heard a rustling sound from behind the door. A shadow appeared from underneath it, and I sensed someone staring at me from the peephole. It was Frank.

"How can I help you?" he asked.

"It's Michael Stern. I'm just dropping off the linens that Lucy bought today."

I heard a clicking sound, and then the door opened. Bingo. I guess my name must have been the secret password.

When I walked in, I heard Lucy's voice call out, "Who is it?"

"It's Michael Stern with your order," replied Frank.

"Oh, yes. Bring him in."

Frank escorted me to the dining room, where Lucy and Gary were eating dinner.

Lucy looked at Gary from across the table. "You know Michael, right? He's my number-one fan."

I smiled to myself. It never got old, hearing her say that.

*   *   *

The next day I received a personal call from Gary; he wanted white towels for his bathroom, and he was very particular about it.

"These white towels—they have to be the right kind of feel, you know what I mean?" Gary asked.

I nodded, even though I knew he couldn't see me nodding. "Okay, well, here's what I'll do. I'll purchase one large white towel from every brand that we carry. That way, you can pick exactly what it is you want."

Gary liked the sound of that, and the next day, I drove over to their house in the evening. This time, I had arrived right before dinner, and they invited me to join them.

As I eagerly took my place at the table, I thought to myself: *How cool is this? I get to eat a Beverly Hills meal with Lucy and Gary.*

Visions of lobster and steak danced in my head. Needless to say, I was pretty surprised when they handed me a paper plate and passed over a tray of meat loaf! It turned out that it was their maid's day off, and meat loaf was all they had available.

We took our dinner into Gary's den, setting our plates down on TV trays. While we ate, we watched *Wheel of Fortune*. I got a kick out of listening to Lucy yell at the television throughout the show.

"Buy a vowel! Buy a vowel!" she screamed as her plate of meat loaf grew colder and colder in front of her.

After dinner, Lucy gave me her home phone number. "Please call me next week when you're off, and we'll play backgammon."

I told her I would. How could I say no to that?

Before I left, Gary examined all the towels I had brought over, and in no time, he picked one out from the bunch. Now I knew what to buy for him. I promised that I would be back soon with a dozen towels. I told them that I would use my employee discount, so that they would receive 20 percent off. They were absolutely thrilled.

From that point on, they called me whenever they needed anything from the linens department. I was thrilled to be their go-to guy. I felt as if I had been welcomed into their circle somehow.

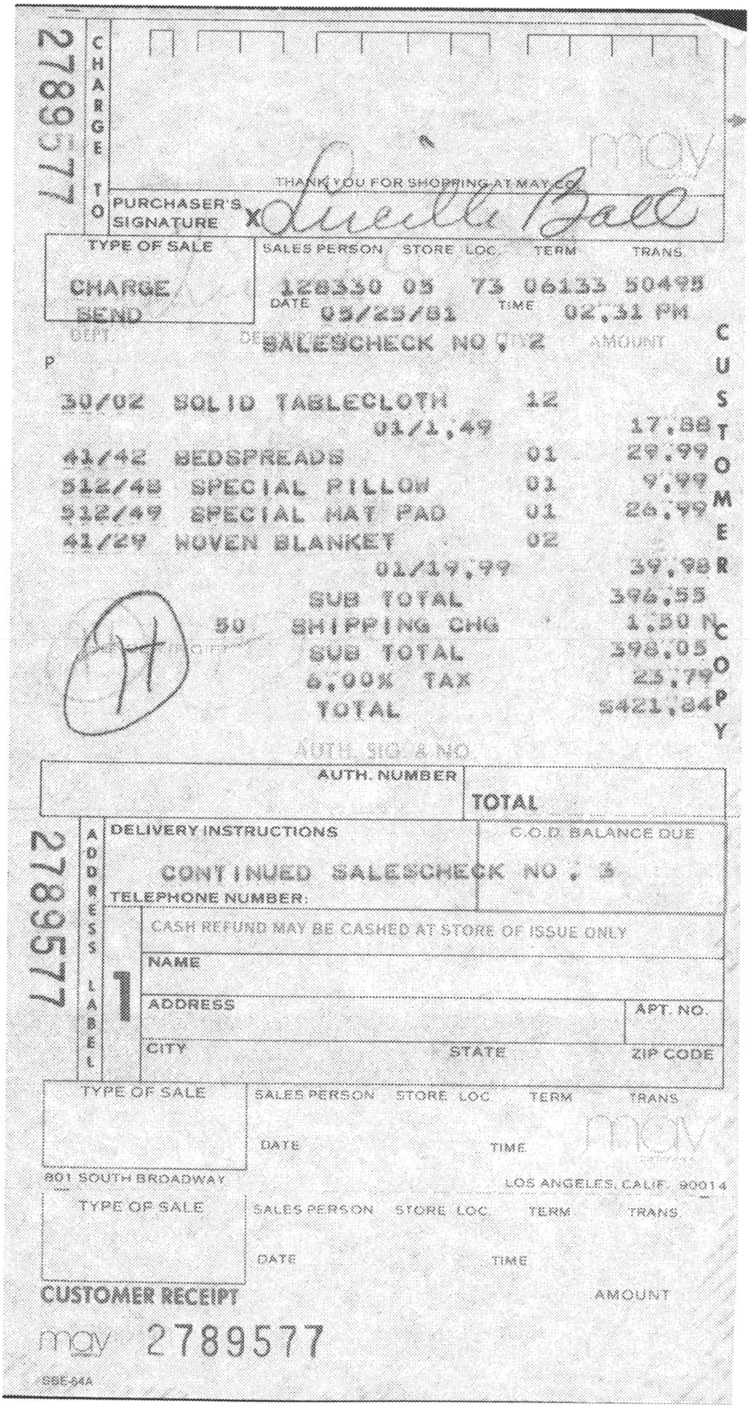

2789577

CHARGE TO

THANK YOU FOR SHOPPING AT MAY CO.

PURCHASER'S SIGNATURE X Lucille Ball

TYPE OF SALE	SALES PERSON	STORE LOC.	TERM	TRANS.
CHARGE SEND	128330	05	73 06133	50495

DATE 05/25/81 TIME 02.31 PM

SALESCHECK NO. 2

30/02	SOLID TABLECLOTH	12	
	01/1.49		17.88
41/42	BEDSPREADS	01	29.99
512/48	SPECIAL PILLOW	01	9.99
512/49	SPECIAL MAT PAD	01	26.99
41/29	WOVEN BLANKET	02	
	01/19.99		39.98
	SUB TOTAL		396.55
50	SHIPPING CHG		1.50
	SUB TOTAL		398.05
	6.00% TAX		23.79
	TOTAL		$421.84

CUSTOMER COPY

AUTH. NUMBER

TOTAL

DELIVERY INSTRUCTIONS

C.O.D. BALANCE DUE

CONTINUED SALESCHECK NO. 3

TELEPHONE NUMBER:

ADDRESS LABEL

CASH REFUND MAY BE CASHED AT STORE OF ISSUE ONLY

NAME

ADDRESS

APT. NO.

CITY STATE ZIP CODE

TYPE OF SALE SALES PERSON STORE LOC. TERM TRANS.

DATE TIME

801 SOUTH BROADWAY LOS ANGELES, CALIF. 90014

TYPE OF SALE SALES PERSON STORE LOC. TERM TRANS.

DATE TIME

CUSTOMER RECEIPT AMOUNT

may 2789577

The receipt from the May Co. department store

CHAPTER 25

Determining what to get Lucy for her birthday or for Christmas was a struggle unlike any other. The woman had just about everything. And if there was something she didn't have, it was probably because she had no interest in owning it.

In the beginning of my friendship with Lucy, I gifted her on special occasions with place mats, a purse, and a picture frame. Every time I went to buy something for Lucy, my mind tangled itself in knots trying to come up with ideas for things that nobody would have ever thought to give her.

Well, one day in April of '83, the perfect opportunity smacked into me, headfirst. Actress Bette Davis was signing her brand-new record album—*Miss Bette Davis Sings*—at a record store in Hollywood. I knew that Bette Davis had gone to the same acting school as Lucy. Also, during the Lucy-Desi comedy hours—in the episode "The Star Next Door"—Miss Davis had been set to appear. However, she had to back out at the last minute and was replaced by Tallulah Bankhead instead.

This would be the perfect opportunity to get Lucy something that she probably doesn't have, I thought to myself.

I waited in line for three hours until it was my turn. I asked Miss Davis to sign two records for me—one for myself and one for Lucy.

Unable to keep it to myself, I mentioned to Miss Davis that it was going to be a gift for Lucy, and she said, in the way only Bette Davis could, "Why would Lucille want *this*?"

I shrugged, not quite knowing how to answer that question. Besides, I thought it was a pretty good gift idea, considering how Lucy knew her and all.

Miss Davis signed the album to "Lucille," even though I had called her

"Lucy." It wasn't something that I was incredibly disappointed about, just something I noticed.

I drove over to Lucy's house to drop off the record, and upon seeing it, she burst into laughter. She thought it was a riot that Bette would ever do that type of album.

After the laughter was out of the way, Lucy thanked me for the record and promised that she would listen to it.

About five months later, while I was over at Lucy's place, she surprised me by handing back the Bette Davis record. Before I could ask her what was going on, she said to me, "Michael, I know you collect autographs so here's Bette Davis's autograph on a record that she did years ago."

I froze, clutching the record in my hand. Should I …?

"Oh, thanks," I responded, looking down at the album, pretending to be impressed.

I didn't want to embarrass her by reminding her that I had given her the album only several months ago, so I kept my mouth shut! I guess she wasn't too crazy about the gift.

Some time later, Lucy also ended up donating the place mats I had given her to the Children's World charity that I volunteered for.

I learned early on that Lucy really didn't need anything material from me. She appreciated other things. Our friendship with each other was enough for her. She was also grateful for cards on special occasions.

My mom was famous for her cheesecakes, so I asked her to make one for Lucy and Gary, and one for Wanda, for the holidays one year. The idea was genius. Soon after receiving their cakes, Lucy and Wanda each sent my mom a glowing thank-you card. Lucy even phoned my mom to tell her how much she and Gary liked the cheesecake.

Finally, I had discovered the way to Lucy's heart. It was her sweet tooth!

CHAPTER 26

I wasn't the only avid Lucy collector. Believe it or not, Lucy also loved to collect things of herself. Although she didn't care to collect everything, she lived for discovering those rare items that were difficult to get just anywhere. Case in point: that paperback book I had wanted her to sign after class that one night. That was a special item, and she wasted no time claiming it for herself!

One day during the summer of '83, while I was at her house playing backgammon, she said to me, "If you ever see a magazine with me on it called *Lions Roar*, pick it up. It's from MGM Studios, and I was on the cover years ago."

I quickly sped through the file cabinet in my brain, trying to remember if I had ever come across that magazine before. But nothing came up.

"It's probably impossible to find. I've never seen that magazine before," I told Lucy, shrugging my shoulders.

And then, not wanting to disappoint her completely, I added, "I'll keep my eyes open for it, though."

That conversation was held on a Tuesday.

On Thursday, my friend Darin and I were in Hollywood at a memorabilia shop that sold old scripts, autographed pictures, posters, and other movie-related items. We paced through the musty aisles, losing ourselves in the lore of old cinema.

At one point, I noticed the woman who worked there was putting together a display in a glass case. Curious, I walked toward it, peering into the case. And staring back at me was *Lion's Roar* with—you guessed it—Lucille Ball on the cover. The photo was from the 1944 movie *Ziegfeld Follies*.

I stared at the magazine for a moment, unable to believe my luck. Or, more accurately, Lucy's luck.

The price tag for the magazine was seventy-five dollars.

Since going through Wanda was always an easier way of getting to Lucy, I immediately called her at the office. Wanda patched me directly to Lucy, and in mere seconds, Lucy was saying hello on the other end.

In response, I called out, "Eureka! I found it."

"Found what?"

"*Lions Roar*. It's seventy-five dollars."

I could feel excitement surging from the other end of the phone to mine. Lucy was absolutely thrilled.

"I've wanted this for years and years. Yes, please get it! I'll pay you back. And come on over right away."

"My friend Darin is with me. Would that be okay?"

"Sure."

After we disengaged, I went right to work. I grabbed hold of the magazine, brought it up to the cashier, and plucked out my checkbook. I didn't have credit cards in those days, and I wasn't the type to just carry seventy-five dollars in cash on me.

The woman behind the counter looked down at my checkbook and frowned. "Sorry. We don't take personal checks."

I had to think fast. Lucy was waiting on me, and I wasn't about to let this opportunity slip though my fingers.

Leaving Darin behind as a hostage so that no one else would buy the magazine, I raced to the closest bank.

Breathless, I approached the teller with my check, asking him to cash it.

Looking down at the check, the teller shook his head from side to side. "Its from a different bank. We can't cash it."

He informed me that my bank was about two blocks down the street, and within a split second, I was en route to it, jogging over there, worried that somehow I wouldn't make it.

Lucy's words, "come right over," were ringing through my head, and I felt obligated to get there as quickly as I could. I never liked to keep her waiting.

About half an hour later, cash in hand, I went back to the memorabilia shop and released Darin from captivity. I purchased *Lion's Roar*, and we darted out of the shop, intent on making it to Lucy's house as soon as we could.

When we arrived at the house on Roxbury Drive that I had become so familiar with, Frank greeted us at the door.

"Lucy's expecting you. Come on into the den," Frank said, politeness sharpening his every syllable.

Frank asked Darin to wait in the foyer, as Lucy wasn't properly dressed.

When I stepped into the den, I found her there, wearing a white terrycloth bathrobe. Her hair was hidden under a thick scarf, and her face was pale and devoid of makeup.

She must have noticed that I was taking in her unadorned appearance, because her first words to me were, "Well, now, Michael. I guess you see me the way I really am."

Lucy was sitting in a chair across from her friend Thelma Orloff. The two were engaged in a game of backgammon. In a few short hours, Lucy was to head out for the evening and celebrate Milton Berle's seventy-fifth birthday. Despite all that was going on, she was enthusiastic about receiving the magazine.

Lucy turned to Thelma. "I've been looking for this for years."

She explained to Thelma how she had given me the mission to locate this magazine for her only two days ago.

And now here it was. In her hands.

To Lucy, I was a hero of sorts. I had accomplished the impossible, overcome the insurmountable. And the gratitude pouring out of her was tremendous.

Lucy held the magazine up for Thelma to see. Then she opened it and started flipping through the pages with such reverence, as if the magazine were just hot off the presses.

I stood back, watching them, a half smile on my face. It was like watching two giddy schoolgirls. They were both eyeing each page with such respect. It was as if the magazine were some holy shrine that deserved to be worshipped.

Although I didn't want to ruin Lucy's good time, I had to interrupt and remind her about the money she owed me. And instead of just pulling out the money and paying me back, a Lucy Ricardo-esque episode ensued.

Lucy discovered that she only had about forty dollars in cash on her. She was thirty-five dollars short and had to borrow money from both Thelma and Frank to pay me back. (I guess she never carried mad money with her!)

Looking back, I guess I could have waited and that she could have sent me a check in the mail.

Some people might be thinking, *If you were such a big fan, you should have bought the magazine for her!*

I gladly would have if I could have, but at the time, seventy-five dollars was a lot of money for me. It was half the check from my job. Besides, Lucy would have never wanted me to purchase it for her. She was a classy, thoughtful lady and would have never accepted such a gift from a kid like me.

When she walked me to the front door, she saw my friend Darin sitting there. A look of surprise painted Lucy's face. "I forgot you were coming with Michael! You could have come in and said hello."

Then she gave both of us a kiss good-bye, and we left her house.

Mission accomplished.

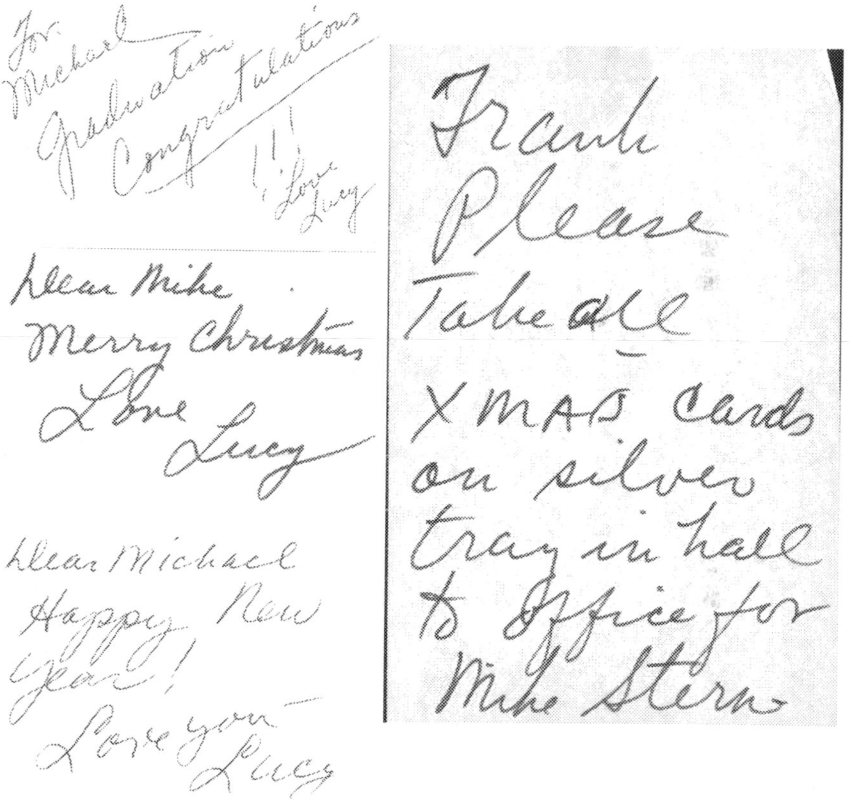

For
Michael
Graduation
Congratulations
! !
Love
Lucy

Dear Mike
Merry Christmas
Love
Lucy

Dear Michael
Happy New
Year !
Love you —
Lucy

Frank
Please
Take all
—
XMAS cards
on silver
tray in hall
to office for
Mike Stern

Notes from Lucy …

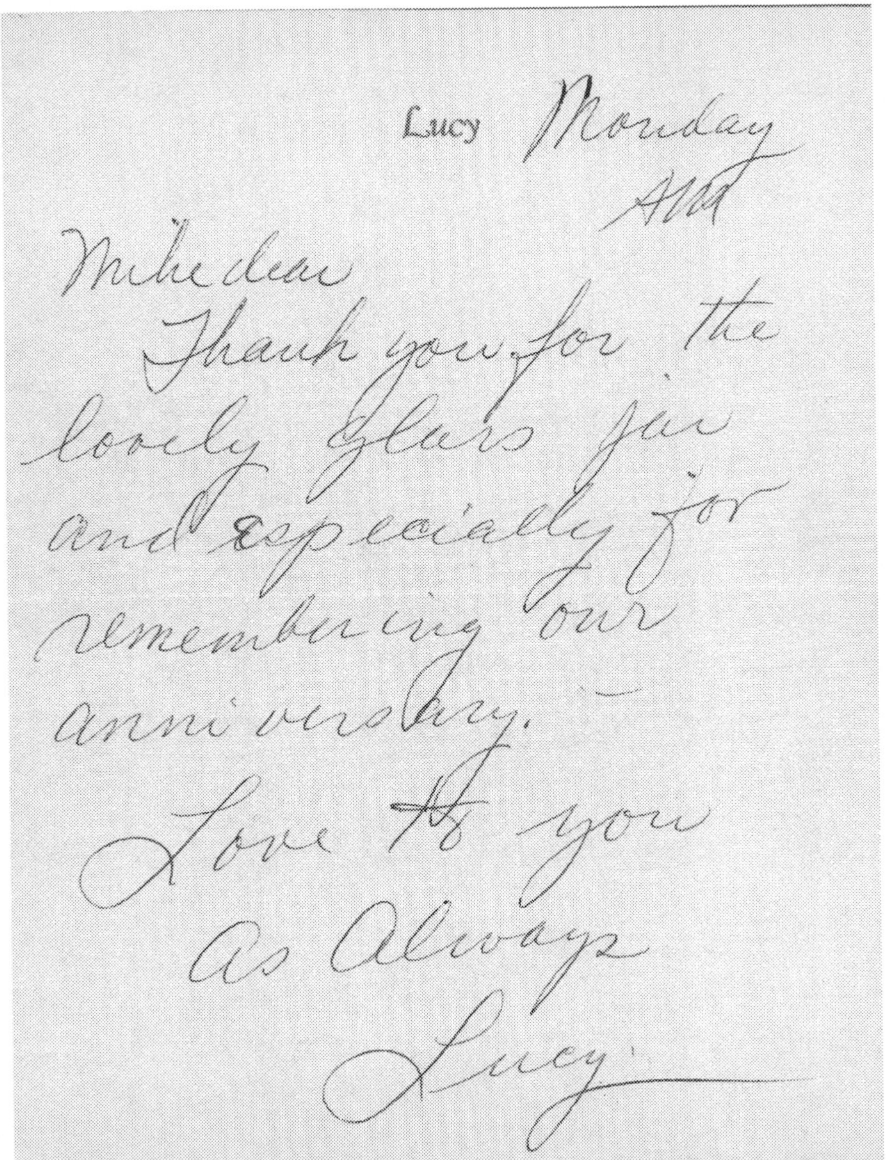

Lucy Monday
AM

Mike dear

Thank you for the
lovely glass jar
and especially for
remembering our
anniversary. —

Love to you
As Always

Lucy

Michael dear—
You know how very
proud of you, I am!
And happy for your
parents — they too
must feel as I do.
Glad to hear you
have your own apt.
Hope this fits in —
Love
     as always
          Lucy

CHAPTER 27

Each year, in honor of Lucy's birthday, the local FOX station would have an *I Love Lucy* birthday marathon. The marathons would feature twelve to sixteen hours of nonstop *I Love Lucy* episodes, back to back. At the beginning of each show, a celebrity would give Lucy a birthday greeting. A variety of people took part in delivering their well wishes for another great year. People like Lucie Arnaz, Desi Jr., Carol Burnett, Betty White, Don Rickles, Whoopi Goldberg, and Lily Tomlin.

A few days before the special marathon was to air on August 6 of 1983, Lucy called me on the phone and invited me over to her place. She proposed a lively day of backgammon playing and marathon watching. Needless to say, I was completely and utterly *in*. I happened to be off work, so there were no commitments holding me back.

That Saturday I arrived at Lucy's house around 1:00 p.m. We ate homemade mac and cheese in her workout room, which was complete with a ballet bar and a few exercise machines. While we ate, we watched episode after episode, indulging in one another's company.

In the past, Lucy had always talked about how she really didn't remember too many of the *I Love Lucy* shows, but after sitting with her that afternoon, I begged to differ. Lucy always remembered. She knew what the show was about either from the first scene or the first couple of scenes. Mind you, she had done these shows some thirty years before. Sometimes she knew what episode it was before I did. We were watching episode 111, which was entitled, "First Stop." In that episode, the Ricardos and the Mertzes stop to spend the night in a cabin next to the train tracks while on their way to California.

In this episode that was airing on the marathon, we discovered that a vital scene had been cut. In the scene, Ethel enters the bathroom to get ready for bed when, all of a sudden, a train comes roaring by. It shakes the entire cabin, filling everyone with worry about how Ethel is doing. Instead of showing that scene, the episode jumped to the part when Ethel exits, her face covered with toothpaste.

Upon seeing this, Lucy was absolutely livid. They had chopped out the scene that explained what had just happened. Great passion ringing through her voice, Lucy said that she was going to call the station and complain. But she knew better than to call and make a fuss of it.

Instead, she walked me over to Gary's office library. In it were copies of all her shows. As everything was in its proper place, Lucy was able to quickly pull out an uncut version of the show. She wanted me to see the scene that had been cut.

Throughout the day, I sneaked looks at her every now and then. I saw that she was paying extra-close attention to the performances of Desi, Vivian, and William. She never laughed at herself, but enjoyed watching and laughing at the others.

Watching *I Love Lucy* while sitting next to Lucy was like nothing I had ever experienced. She told me all kinds of stories. Stories about how Bill Frawley and Fred Mertz were very much the same character. Stories about Viv, and how if she ever needed anything, Bill was always the first to help her out. It was more of a love-hate relationship and not nearly as bad as what had been written about the two. I listened to every story with interest and fascination, aware of just how lucky I was to be getting a live actor's commentary on a show that I had watched and admired for years.

Throughout the day, the doorbell would not stop ringing. Frank was on his feet for most of the day, answering the door. Deliveries of flowers from numerous fans filled the house until it looked like a rose garden. By the end of the night, it looked as if she had more flowers in her house than the local florist.

One of the birthday greetings we watched on television came from me. When the moment arrived, I straightened my spine and leaned toward the television, eager to see that I had not been cut. On the screen I said something like, "Hi Lucy, it's Michael, your number-one fan. Wishing you a very happy birthday."

Lucy eyes became wet with emotion, and she got up on her feet, moving toward me. I hadn't told her that I had shot that piece, as I didn't want her to be disappointed if they didn't air it. She was quite surprised.

"That was very sweet of you," she said, giving me a little thank-you kiss.

The FOX station would always send Lucy the birthday greetings on one tape, just in case she had missed one or two. It was nice to know that, among all the greetings, mine would be there too, and she would have it, always.

At about 5:00 p.m., Gary came home. He had been at the golf course all day. It was nice to see them both together. The first thing he did after he walked through the door was give Lucy the biggest kiss. From one hundred miles away, anyone could see that they were in love. The way they acted around each other, it was as if they were still dating, still experiencing the newness and excitement of a new love.

It was time for me to leave.

"Thanks for a wonderful day, Lucy."

"I hope to see you again," Lucy responded.

She walked me to the door, as she always did. Then she told me to drive safely, and that she loved me.

And with that, I hopped off the porch and made my way toward the car. As I drove off, I wondered how it was possible that such a simple day spent indoors with Lucy could be so precious and amazing.

CHAPTER 28

A good-looking twenty-one-year-old kid by the name of Tom Cruise was just about to take Hollywood by storm. With just a few movies under his belt and the buzz of acclaim all around him, it was obvious that Tom's future was indeed bright. Gary took notice and offered him the lead role in a movie being produced by Lucille Ball Productions. Tom was to play Stefen Djordjevic, the high school star quarterback in the film *All the Right Moves*.

The movie was shot entirely on location in Pennsylvania. Lucy never went to the location. Yet, along with Gary, she was billed as the executive producer of the film, only to have her name removed from the credits later. Because the film turned out to be rated *R*, and contained brief nudity with Tom, Lucy did not want her fans to think it was a family film.

On October 20, 1983, a small premiere of *All the Right Moves* was held on the back lot of 20th Century Fox studios, where Lucy and Gary had their new production office. As this was one of the first movies starring Tom Cruise, it was quite a low-key red-carpet event. No screaming fans or *Entertainment Tonight* involved—just the entire cast and crew coming together to watch the film. Even Lucy and Gary didn't attend.

After the movie, my eyes darted around the room, trying to catch a glimpse of Tom Cruise. I wanted to get his autograph. However, it was difficult locating him; he seemed to just blend in with everyone else.

Finally, my friend had to take me by the hand and walk me over to Tom, saying to the soon-to-be megastar, "Will you tell my friend Michael that you're the guy from the movie?"

I felt so bad that even after seeing the movie, I didn't recognize him. He looked like any other young guy. Good thing he was so cool about it.

I can tell you now that if he walked by me today, I would recognize him immediately.

For years I always wondered if Tom had ever met Lucy. Finally, in February of 2008, I was at the Screen Actors Guild Awards, and Tom was there as well. I went up to him and asked the question that had been bugging me for years. Well, he couldn't have been nicer. He told me that he had never met her, and that was his biggest regret. He had always wanted to call her and thank her for hiring him, but he had been too shy to pick up the phone.

"I grew up watching Lucy," Tom told me, his eyes lit with the glow of nostalgia.

I told him that I talked to Lucy's daughter all the time. He asked for her phone number so that he could call her and thank her. His love and respect for Lucy were palpable.

In fact, I heard that Tom Cruise moved his production company into the old Desilu bungalow soon after Lucy passed away. His company occupied that space for about ten years, and during that time, Tom didn't bother himself with redesigning any of it.

He kept it just the way it was.

CHAPTER 29

It was a Saturday, January 21, 1984. That day marked the first time that the TV Hall of Fame was introduced by the television academy. There were seven inductees—Milton Berle, Paddy Chayefsky, Norman Lear, Edward R. Murrow, William S. Paley, David Sarnoff, and the one lone woman, Lucille Ball.

Lucy was able to get me two tickets for the general audience seating. I asked my brother-in-law's sister, Marilyn, to accompany me that night, and she gladly obliged. The first half of the audience consisted of celebrities sitting at round tables, with plates of food in front of them, while the rest of us were in the back of the house, watching all the stars eat.

That night I managed to get some great autographs and pictures with Barbara Walters, Carol Burnett, and Henry Winkler. The event was black-tie, and this time I came prepared in my rented black-tie attire. After the first twenty minutes of the show, we crashed the celebrity seating and found seats close to Lucy. It was a very emotional night, complete with a variety of Lucy clips filling the screen.

Lucy received very high accolades from Desi Jr., who had the honor of introducing the segment. He introduced Lucie (via tape from New York), who sang a song that she cowrote; it was called "My Mother the Star." After that, Carol Burnett told the audience that same story about the night Lucy came to see her in *Once Upon a Mattress*.

Once the show was over, the Lucy group went out to dinner to Chasen's Restaurant in Beverly Hills, a place that was world famous for its chili. It was one of the most expensive and elegant restaurants in town. I had my own table with Marilyn, Lucy's dear friends were sitting across from me at another table, and Lucy and Gary were sitting at yet another table with Marvin and Barbara Davis.

The waiter welcomed all of us and revealed the specials of the night.

Before ordering, I asked how much an item on the menu was, and the waiter's forehead scrunched up into a question mark. He had to ask two or three people who worked at the restaurant in order to find out the price. I guess if you can go to Chasen's, you probably aren't all that concerned about what the price is. Marilyn ordered a chicken dish and a side of broccoli. (Everything was à la carte.) She also asked to have some hollandaise sauce on the broccoli. By the way, the broccoli with hollandaise alone came out to a whopping fourteen dollars! To this day, I always kid Marilyn about this.

Although we were at separate tables, there was no shortage of contact with Lucy. In fact, she came to my table no less than three times. One time it was to smoke. Another time to tell me what to eat and how to have them prepare my meal. She advised me to order the steak and to have it butterflied. A butterfly in my steak was not something I had ever had before, but if Lucy liked it, that was good enough for me. When my plate came out, I learned that a butterfly steak is a steak that is split in half and cooked. To this day, I always have my steak butterflied in Lucy's honor.

The third time Lucy approached my table, it was to try a forkful of my chocolate cake dessert, which she had encouraged me to order.

That night was the Night of All Nights. For those couple of hours, I was a celebrity in my own mind, wining and dining with the best of them. Looking around at other tables, I spotted people like John Travolta, Marilu Henner, and Lana Turner. To be sitting and eating among them was an honor unlike any other. At Chasen's, I felt like an absolute star. The night was a wonderful success. To this day I still remind Marilyn of the time we had.

CHAPTER 30

Lucy had a way of making me feel that she was my second mother.

One time she gave me an unexpected lesson about AIDS. We were sitting and playing backgammon in her home when I told her that my cousin Larry had just died of cancer.

"I'm sorry to hear that," Lucy responded. Then, "Was it AIDS?"

I shook my head. "No, he wasn't gay. He was married, had two young kids."

From there Lucy took a deep breath and delved into a stern lesson on AIDS. Wanting to clear up any misconceptions I had, she told me that one didn't have to be gay to have AIDS. She actually knew more about the disease than I did. Here I was, a twenty-three-year-old kid, getting a thorough and rigorous lecture about AIDS from my seventy-three-year-old celebrity friend.

She was so informed and well read. As it was the early eighties, AIDS was not really talked about.

A year later Rock Hudson passed away, and Lucy was really depressed about his death. She had known him for almost forty years.

"He died way before his time," she told me, the wetness in her eyes revealing the emotion inside her.

*   *   *

Lucy couldn't help but exercise her motherly instincts. I was a kid, and she was always looking out for me.

One day, after countless hours of playing backgammon, I decided it was time to leave Lucy's place and head home. It was around 6:00 p.m. The weather was a bit chilly, because of the strength of the wind on that day.

141

As I prepared to leave, Lucy's eyes studied me rather closely. Then she asked, "Michael, where's your jacket?"

"I didn't bring one."

A cloud of disapproval fell over Lucy's face. "Why didn't you bring a jacket? It's cold."

"I'm going right to my car."

Having none of that, Lucy turned toward the hallway. "Let me see what I have."

Before I could protest, Lucy zipped over to the hall closet and pulled out a "members-only" kind of jacket. Holding it up in front of me, Lucy urged, "Put this on. It's Desi's."

"I'm only going to my car and then right home."

But Lucy would not budge. She was like a mother who was talking to a seven-year-old.

"Now, Michael. Put on this jacket before you go out to your car."

Lucy was a persistent woman, and I was no match against her. So I gave in.

"Yes, Lucy," I responded, taking the jacket from her.

If I had tried to say no again, she probably would have sent me to my room for the rest of the night!

The next time I came over to play backgammon, I brought back Desi's jacket. And this time, I made sure to bring my own jacket. It's funny because now I never leave my house without a jacket. I always have a spare in my trunk.

I guess it's not such a bad thing, having a mother (or second mother) to look out for you.

CHAPTER 31

About forty miles south of Los Angeles, Lucy held another Q&A discussion at Claremont College. From friends like Cary Grant and Dick Shawn, Lucy had learned that she could set up gigs speaking to people throughout the country. Lucy held these discussions in New York, Florida, and California. She could have done them every night, all over the world, if she'd had the appetite for it.

It was November of 1985. The fans came by in droves to see her at Claremont. Tickets to the event were twenty dollars each, and the 2,494-seat auditorium sold out within a day. About an hour before the start of the event, Lucy, Gary, Darin, and I all sat in one large room that acted as a makeup room, dressing room, and green room. Tom Watson was there also. He was (and still is) president of the We Love Lucy fan club. He became Lucy's publicist and assistant after Howard McClay passed away in the late seventies. Tom is the absolute expert on just about anything that is Lucy-related. His mind is like a tremendous file cabinet, complete with facts, vivid memories, and wonderful stories. To this day, we remain friends, and it's a pleasure to have him in my life.

In the makeup room/dressing room/green room, there was an abundance of food for all of us to enjoy. The president of Claremont College and his wife joined in on the act as well, chatting with us and making sure everyone was comfortable.

There were countless flower deliveries from fans. By the end of the night, it looked like a funeral parlor. Fans just loved to send Lucy flowers.

Gary put together a thirty-minute clip wheel from all of Lucy's TV shows for the opening segment of the Q&A.

It was almost deafening to hear 2,494 people laughing at Vitameatavegamin and the Candy Factory scenes. There was an energy in the air—an energy that was full of warmth and buzz and rambunctious vibration.

Watching *I Love Lucy* on a forty-foot screen was incredibly amazing. Everyone was truly engaged and wrapped up in all that was unfolding on the screen. It was almost as if all the people in the auditorium had never seen the shows before. Experiencing the shows in this way really allowed me to see everything in a new light, to look at the clips with a fresh eye. It was truly an experience.

Lucy came out to a standing ovation. One of the first questions that someone in the audience asked was, "How does it feel to be an American legend?"

Lucy's answer?

"To be American *anything* is such an honor."

After ninety minutes whizzed by, the show was over.

We all went back to the green room, where Lucy greeted a few friends and college dignitaries. I helped Lucy and Gary pack everything up. There was no way that Lucy and Gary were going to be able to take all the flowers home. Lucy collected all the cards and gave two very large bouquets of flowers to the president and his wife, who were absolutely delighted.

Darin and I helped load Gary's car with as many bouquets of flowers as we could. Once it was completely full, we loaded about—*I kid you not!*—twenty-five dozen bouquets into my car.

"Why don't you give a bouquet to your mother?" Lucy suggested. "The rest you should give to a hospital."

I decided to escort Lucy to her car, as usual. Right when we exited, fifty eager fans were waiting for her. She signed autographs for everyone, on things like posters, pictures, baseballs, and pieces of paper. Not only that, but Lucy received even more flowers to add to her overflowing collection.

After Lucy and Gary left, Darin and I got into my car to go home. No sooner had I got behind the wheel than I was sneezing. I was allergic to all the flowers. Thinking it would pass, I started driving and got onto the freeway toward home. But my sneezing only intensified. I saw a sign that read "Hospital." Unable to take the sneezing anymore, I pulled off the freeway and drove right up to Loma Linda Children's Hospital. It was close to midnight.

The nurses were thrilled to be receiving such a gift. They gladly accepted all the flowers and were happy to know they were from Lucy.

"These will make all the rooms very cheery," one of the nurses told me, gratitude infusing every word.

It felt amazing to give away these flowers, to know that they would be brightening up every room they were present in. Lucy always came up with the greatest ideas.

CHAPTER 32

Over the years, Lucy gave me items that she thought I would like—especially ones with autographs on them. During this time, I learned the full meaning of the phrase "One man's junk is another man's treasure."

One of the craziest items she offered me was an old leg cast. She had used it when she broke her leg skiing in Colorado in the early seventies. The plaster of paris walking cast had actually been seen on the *Here's Lucy* shows. Lucy had been cleaning her storage unit when she came upon the old item. She gazed at the cast, trying to figure out exactly what to do with it.

Hold onto it? Throw it out?

But then she thought of me.

She autographed it and presented it to me one day, saying, "Now you have the cast from *I Love Lucy*."

That same day she also gave me a movie poster of her and Bob Hope from the movie *Fancy Pants*. She told me that it was one of her favorite movies she had done with Bob.

"This poster was used on a *Dinah Shore Show* when I was a guest. And after the show, they gave it to me," Lucy said as she placed the poster in my possession.

I also received another special item from her, one that I am so honored to have—the special Emmy she received from the television academy on her thirtieth anniversary on television. It was a certificate that was signed by attendees of that year's award ceremony, including autographs from people like Betty White, Ed Asner, Shirley MacLaine, Peter O'Toole, Gary Coleman, Tony Danza, and Rod Steiger. It is an amazing treasure and piece of history that I am honored to have in my Lucy collection.

In 1977, Lucy gave me another special item—the first annual Women in

Film award, which honors dynamic women in film and television. In 1994, the Women in Film organization set up a special award called the Lucy Award. Past winners include Carol Burnett, Roseanne Barr, Debra Messing, Megan Mullally, Rosie O'Donnell, Cher, Ellen Degeneres, Sharon Stone, Barbara Walters, Sarah Jessica Parker, Marlo Thomas, Angela Lansbury, and Imogene Coca. The only female writer for Lucy's shows, Madelyn Pugh Davis, was also a recipient of this award.

Another item I received from Lucy was an 11 x 14 framed picture that was on the *Here's Lucy* set when Flip Wilson was a guest. It's a picture of Flip, and it reads, "To Lucy & Gary/I Love Lucy/Flip Wilson."

*　　　　*　　　　*

Every year Lucy and Gary attended the Carousel Ball in Denver, Colorado, which was hosted by their good friends Marvin and Barbara Davis. One year, Lucy purchased a Chrysler LeBaron car at the charity auction. Now, before you jump out of your seat thinking that Lucy purchased this car for me, I have to (unfortunately) say that it wasn't so.

However, the following year, she did bid on and win a poster that was signed by all those attending the event, including celebrities like Henry Kissinger, Gerald and Betty Ford, Raquel Welch, Cary Grant, Arnold Schwarzenegger, and about fifty other top talents. And she gave the poster to me!

But back to that time when Lucy purchased the convertible ...

When the Chrysler LeBaron was delivered, I was actually at Lucy's home. Within moments of its arrival, Frank got right down to business, showing Lucy how to work the car. I had never seen anything else like it. The car had voice activation, and whenever the door was slightly open, it would say, in a stern and serious voice, "The door is ajar."

And Lucy would say right back, "No, it's a door, not a jar."

Lucy was doing a Lucy episode right before my eyes.

The voice would then say something else, and Lucy would again talk right back to it, engaging with it.

It became absolutely hysterical.

That very day, Lucy drove me around the block in her new car. It was the only time Lucy ever drove me around. At one point, I was tempted to ask her if she had called in and got her car insurance—just like Lucy Ricardo had to do the day she received her convertible.

I rested my back against the passenger seat, enjoying every minute of our spontaneous ride. That afternoon she gave me a personal tour of the stars' homes, taking me all around town.

I was driving with Miss Lucy, and it felt pretty damn good.

*   *   *

The first gift I ever received from Lucy for the holidays was a pewter cup and plate that read, "Love, Lucy & Gary." She also gave me the first Lucy collector plate and a *Here's Lucy* doll by Effanbee. Through the years, there were other gifts, including bottles of wine, watches, and clocks.

"You could always use an extra clock or watch," Lucy told me on more than one occasion.

One watch that she gave me was in a Van Cleef and Arpels box. Now let me just say, for those who don't know—Van Cleef and Arpels is one of the most expensive jewelers in Beverly Hills. Seeing my watch in this box got my heart rate going.

How much did Lucy actually spend on this?

It seemed that an investigation of sorts was in order. The black watch was a Dynasty watch. My friend Darin called Van Cleef for me and asked how much a Dynasty watch went for. The person on the other end of the line told him that a watch like that would cost about fifty-four thousand dollars.

When Darin reported the number back to me, I scratched my head. *Really?* I knew Lucy loved me, but not *that* much.

So I put Darin to work once again. Like the good friend that he is, he did some more research and found that my watch was worth about one hundred dollars. It seemed that Lucy had just put it in a Van Cleef box! (Ethel Mertz did the same thing with a cigarette lighter from an *I Love Lucy* episode.)

Mystery solved.

In 1986, Lucy had these watches made for everyone on the *Life with Lucy* crew. The watch had a round face, complete with a perfectly drawn caricature of Lucy and the words "Love, Lucy."

Lucy gave me one of these watches, and I still wear it every single day. Whenever I look down at my wrist for the time, I can't help but think of her.

Lucy also gave me some fun gifts that I'll always cherish. One of them was an oversized brown beach towel that Liza Minnelli had given Desi Jr. On it are the words "Liza Loves Desi."

"Well," Lucy said, shrugging, "I guess Desi won't be using this any longer."

Every January, Lucy was kind enough to give me all the celebrity Christmas cards that she had received. I would snatch them up eagerly and then put them on display in my house, almost as if I were the one who had actually received all the cards from those big-name celebrities. There were cards from people like Carol Burnett, Sammy Davis Jr., Don Rickles, and Julio Iglesias. She had even received cards from Presidents Ford, Carter, and Bush Sr.!

During one of my birthdays, I remember buying myself a gold "Oscar" charm. I showed it to Lucy and told her that I had bought it out of a man's briefcase and that it cost me only twenty dollars.

She pulled out twenty dollars from her backgammon table and handed it to me.

"Happy Birthday," Lucy beamed. "I now present you with your gold Oscar."

CHAPTER 33

Lucy and I had a conversation about my employment at the kickoff party for the annual "Television and Radio Museum" event which was held at the Los Angeles County Museum. Guests that night included Jean Stapleton, Linda Lavin, Red Buttons, Hal Linden, Sid Caesar, Rose Marie, Bob Carroll Jr., and Madelyn Pugh Davis.

Mr. Lipton, the store manager at May Company, had decided to leave for Robinson's, a higher end department store, and he took me with him. At first, I transitioned into my new job with great ease. However, after some time, I just wasn't feeling it anymore. Things were changing at the company, and I no longer wanted to stay onboard selling linens. I wanted to quit.

Lucy's eyes became saucers. "Have you talked to your parents about this?"

"No."

"Why are you telling me then? You should talk to your parents first."

Through the years of our friendship, Lucy was always telling me to talk to my parents first. To her, communication was a key part of every relationship. Perhaps that's why she had so many strong and deep bonds with the people in her life. Lucy was one smart person.

"Don't quit. Never be a quitter."

That was a motto that Lucy lived by. And she tried to impress it upon me on that day.

I ended up toughing it out and staying with Robinson's for another two years, moving from linens to women's shoes and then to furniture, where it was all commission sales, which proved to be lucrative.

Lucy, Tom Watson, and I spent most of the night chatting with one another.

Bored by the events of the night, Lucy looked over at me and Tom. "It's always the same food, the same people, and the same speeches every year."

Then Lucy looked down at her plate. "This piece of chicken is definitely from last year."

At one point, I jokingly asked Bob and Madelyn, "If Lucy ever came back to television, would you have stories to write?"

They smiled and told me that this unlikely scenario was one that they didn't have to worry about, since Lucy was retired from television. However, if it *did* happen, their answer would be *yes*.

Well, the next day there was a huge announcement on the news—*Lucy was returning to television*!

Phone calls flooded in from my friends all day, demanding to know all the details about Lucy's return. I hadn't seen the news yet and had absolutely no clue what they were talking about. I told them all that they were mistaken. Told them that I had just seen Lucy the night before and that she hadn't mentioned anything like that.

Boy, was I wrong.

When *Entertainment Tonight* came on television that night, Lucille Ball was the top news story. There on the screen in front of me, I learned that Lucy was spending the next season over at ABC in a new comedy series.

Within seconds after the announcement, Tom and I got on the phone with one another. We were both utterly confused.

"Did we miss anything last night?" Tom asked. "Did she tell you anything privately?"

We were both quite shocked.

There had been not a word from Lucy about this decision the night before. Not even the slightest hint.

I learned later that the news was released to the press earlier than it was supposed to be. Not even Bob and Madelyn knew that she was thinking of returning to television.

One thing was for sure—this was going to be one exciting year!

What I call
"Oh, I am
in the shot"
pictures

Some of the people Lucy worked with who I met along the way ...

With Barbara Walters

With Helen Hayes

With Doris Day

With Carol Burnett

With Dick Van Dyke

With Mary Tyler Moore

With Bob Hope

With Milton Berle

CHAPTER 34

The new ABC series was a joint venture between Aaron Spelling Productions and Lucille Ball Productions. Forty years earlier, Aaron Spelling had been a struggling actor who once appeared as a hillbilly on an *I Love Lucy* episode. Now, four decades later, he was one of the most powerful men in Hollywood, having produced such shows as *Dynasty* and *Charlie's Angels*. He knew that everyone loved Lucy, and that there was great potential for a new series. To pull a seventy-five-year-old out of retirement was unimaginable. But they were able to sell an unwritten series to ABC with no plot whatsoever. Lucy's name was all it took to get the project off the ground.

Wanting desperately to be involved, I approached Gary and asked him for a job.

"What can you do?" he asked, eyeing me closely.

"What do you have open?" I asked him back. "I can do anything."

Gary thought to himself for a moment and then his lips started curving downward. "I don't want you to quit your day job. You never know what can happen in this business."

I walked away from that conversation horribly upset. I wanted nothing more than to work with Lucy. It didn't matter what or how or where. I just knew that I could do it. I could even work part-time, if they had a place for me.

A man on a mission, I went in and talked to the personnel department at Robinson's. Minutes later I emerged from that conversation a happy individual. They told me I could have my days off on Wednesdays and Thursdays, which would be the full rehearsal day and show day of Lucy's new series.

After telling Gary about my days off, that was it. I was immediately part of the team.

On Wednesdays, I hung around with Tom and Lucy, running errands for them. On Thursdays, I was given the guest list for the show and positioned at the main gate, where I was to check off the names of the VIP guests.

In other words, absolute heaven.

I had never, in a million years, pictured myself working with Lucy in this capacity.

*   *   *

With her loyal nature, Lucy was intent upon hiring as many people as she could from her old shows. And so, on *Life with Lucy*, she was once again surrounded by people who had worked with her since the *I Love Lucy* days.

Eighty-year-old Gale Gordon would once again play her beloved sidekick.

"I would not have gone back to television without him," she once said.

Marc Daniels directed the first few episodes, and Bob Carroll Jr. and Madelyn Pugh Davis went on to write or oversee the writing of all the shows. And although he was practically deaf during this point in his life, Cameron McCullough was the sound engineer. Lucy found it very funny and ironic to have a deaf man as the sound engineer. Despite this challenge, he was exceptional at his job.

One of Lucy's secretaries from the past was Theresa Price, another redhead. Now she was working in the *Life with Lucy* office as Gary's assistant. Every time Theresa would answer the phone, her greeting would go on for practically two minutes before it was time for the person on the other end to speak. Theresa's greeting went something like: "Good-morning-Mr.-Morton's-office-of-*Life-With-Lucy*-this-is-Theresa-speaking-how-may-I-help-you-today?"

Lucy thought this was completely hilarious and would imitate Theresa's never-ending greeting all the time in a playful, loving way.

Lucy also brought back performer Larri Thomas, who served as her stand-in. Larri had worked as a stand-in on *Here's Lucy* and several Lucille Ball specials, also appearing on camera in the *Lucy-Desi Comedy Hour*. The show was called "Lucy Wants a Career," and Paul Douglas was the guest star. Larri Thomas was one of the girls who auditioned in that episode as another Girl Friday.

There was another "Larry" on the show—the actor Larry Anderson. He played Ted McGibbon, Lucy's son-in-law.

Life with Lucy was a happy set, free of drama and conflict. As Lucy chose reliable, talented, and hardworking people, she basically set the stage for a smooth show. Everyone got along very well. All of us knew that we were involved in something special, that we had the opportunity to create something unique and full of life. And in return, we got to witness the Queen of Comedy at work.

Lucy loved her new crew from the beginning. She had hired the best of the best to work for her, and she felt confident in their ability to deliver.

Everyone on the set was in absolute awe of her talent. Watching her work was a tremendous pleasure, and it was obvious that all of the cast and crew were so grateful to be a part of this new universe that she had welcomed them into. Lucy was a team player—not a diva—and her mere presence inspired people to work harder, to perform with the fullness of their spirits. Even after years of retirement, Lucy was, without a doubt, still the ultimate Queen of Television.

On the first night of filming (Friday, July 18), Lucie sent her mom three flowers with a note that read, "We will be in the bleachers cheering you on. Love, DeDe, Viv, and Bill."

It was such a touching gesture. Judging by the emotion on Lucy's face after she read the note, the flowers and note meant so much to her.

Minutes before the taping was to start, I studied Lucy's face, looking for any trace of nervousness.

But there was none to be found.

CHAPTER 35

Watching the *Life with Lucy* rehearsals was a blast. Every Wednesday and Thursday, I would stop by the set in the morning, while they were running through their lines. For lunch, Tom, Lucy, and I would take our food to Lucy's dressing room, which was located at the far end of the studio lot. I was always the designated driver, transporting all of us across the lot via golf cart.

Lunch was a great time for Lucy, because it was the one hour of the day that she did not have to be on. Sometimes instead of eating lunch, she would nap; other times, she spent the hour autographing stacks of pictures.

One time Lucy taught us one of her favorite word games, which was almost like Wheel of Fortune meets Scrabble; there were thirty blank squares on a pad of paper, and we had to call out letters, one at a time, and place them on each blank square. Then we would try to come up with words spontaneously.

On one occasion, we were in the process of starting a new game. Lucy began by calling out the letter *F*. Tom quickly followed, coming in with the letter *U*. Not wanting to miss out on the opportunity, I came in with the letter *C*.

Before it got any further, Lucy shook her head and said, "Boys, let's not go there."

Tom and I burst out laughing.

There was one occasion in her dressing room that I'll never forget.

During the beginning weeks of *Life with Lucy*, Lucy would sometimes do phone interviews during her lunch breaks to promote the show. One time a woman from Jamestown, New York called to speak with her. Since the woman was from her hometown, Lucy agreed to do the interview. While she was on the phone, Tom and I sat in the room eating our lunch. We could only hear Lucy's end of the conversation, of course. We listened as she spoke about how wonderful it was to be back on weekly television. She spoke of how great it was to work with her costar Gale Gordon again, and to have back her original writers and director.

From our point of view, it seemed as if the interview was going quite well. But all that soon changed.

In the middle of the conversation, Lucy's face seemed to darken. She raised the receiver above her head for a moment and quietly said the word "bitch," so that the interviewer could not hear. Then she brought the receiver back to her ear and continued the interview as if nothing had happened.

About a minute after that, Lucy repeated what she had done the last time, holding the receiver up in the air and saying the word "bitch" again. This time, instead of continuing the conversation, she threw the phone down and started to cry. Before Tom or I could ask what was wrong, Lucy peeled out of the dressing room.

Tom acted quickly, picking up the phone. "Yes. Hello. I'm sorry, but Miss Ball has just been called back to the set."

After disengaging from the interviewer, Tom told me to run and find Lucy. I quickly made my way outside and found her walking down one of the studio streets; she was still in tears.

"What's wrong, Lucy?"

Lucy spoke through the tears, her voice trembling. "The lady on the phone. She kept telling me I was too old. Asking me, 'Why are you even working?'"

I tried to comfort her, assuring her that the lady did not know what she was talking about. But the tears kept flowing. I had never seen Lucy like this.

We passed the mill at the studio, and Lucy muttered that there must be someplace inside where she could kill herself.

I knew that she was just talking. She would never do anything like that. The interviewer's words had cut deep into her, making her feel no longer wanted, no longer needed. For Lucy, this was the worst kind of insult. She didn't feel that seventy-five was too old. She had more energy than most people who were half her age.

What the interviewer had said was unjust; Lucy had revolutionized the face of television, breaking past barriers and finding her way into the homes of millions—not an easy feat. How could an industry that she had given so much of herself to want to throw her away like this?

I got Lucy back to the stage, where she went off to her onstage dressing room to fix herself up. I called Gary, and he immediately drove from his office to make sure Lucy was okay.

When the lunch break was over, Lucy put on a happy face and went onto the set, prepared to work, as if nothing had happened.

She was a trouper at any age.

CHAPTER 36

Show night was always an exciting time for me.

When the rehearsals finished, everyone piled into the neighboring soundstage for a catered dinner. Lucy never ate dinner with the cast, because she was busy getting made up for the show. The process took about *two whole hours*.

Hairstylist, Irma Kusely needed time to do her wigs, and Fred Williams needed time to do her makeup. One day I learned that it was not just her face that needed makeup, but also her hands. The skin on her hands had to match her face as closely as possible. This had to be done with the utmost care.

On top of all that, the stage manager and director also needed some time with Lucy for last-minute notes. Things were busy in Lucy's world, to say the least.

I was always first in line for dinner— not because I was shoving everyone out of the way to eagerly get a plate for myself, but because I still had work to do. I would pick up five complete dinners—one for Lucy, Tom, Irma, the makeup guy, and myself. I would then hightail it over to the large dressing room on the other side of the lot, and we would all scarf the food down in *five* minutes.

That was my lunch break.

After taking my last bite of food, I would dash over to my post at the guard shack to let the VIPs onto the studio lot.

Now, I'll admit it right here and right now—I was the worst at remembering faces. So much so that, after a couple of weeks, if someone sounded like they knew what they were doing, I let them onto the lot. Or even if they knew my name, I figured that it was okay to let them on.

The show had tons of VIPs, including actors Shelley Winters and Barbara

Rush. Lucy's friends from *Mame*—Oscar-winning choreographer Onna White and costumer Theadora Van Runkle—were also on the VIP list. It was quite a task to try to keep up with all the guests and make sure that they were settled.

About thirty minutes before the show was to start, I would make my way to the stage, checking to see that all the VIPs were in the proper seats.

Then, as if he had never taken a break from the spotlight, Gary pounced onto the stage to warm up the audience. Even after all that time away, he still had it. With his magnetic presence, he entertained the crowd for about twenty minutes. Several minutes before the show was to start, I always headed to the backstage area, just to make sure that no additional VIPs were back there.

Gary didn't introduce Lucy before the start of the show, as was done in all her other series. This was a new show, and a new way of doing things was in play.

At the beginning of the very first *Life with Lucy* taping, I was standing next to Lucy. There was about one minute before she had to go on. Unable to sit still, she was bouncing around, waiting for a cue. I gave her a thumbs-up, and she lifted her thumb into the air, returning the gesture.

My work done, I left backstage and went to the bleacher section in the top row, where I watched the show with Tom. It was finally time for me to sit back, relax, and enjoy. My entire body melted into my seat. I couldn't wait to see the show.

When Lucy made her entrance onto the set, the entire studio exploded with applause— applause that seemed to continue and continue, without end. Intermingled with that applause were shouts and cheers. It was as if a bolt of electricity had shot through the room, overtaking everyone and everything.

The actors who played Lucy's daughter and son-in-law—Ann Dusenburry and Larry Anderson—were in a kissing scene on a couch. The funny thing was, they had to *keep* kissing until the applause died down. Their lips were locked for quite some time, as the clapping just wouldn't let up.

The love for Lucy was evident. There was such a natural flow of affection and warmth lilting through the air.

The taping of the first show was a success.

Leaving the set that night, I thought to myself, *This is going to be a hit; no doubt about it.*

Lucy was back in action.

CHAPTER 37

Gary used to get sandwiches from Art's Deli when he worked on *Here's Lucy*.

"It's one of the best delis in California," he told me during one of our conversations.

I knew Art's Deli very well, since it was close to my home, in the San Fernando Valley. I made a mental note of his love for the place, and during the second week of taping, I surprised Gary with a corned beef sandwich from Art's Deli. He absolutely lit up when I gave it to him.

I'll admit, I was engaging in a bit of brownnosing, but I really just wanted to do something nice for him. He had given me such an amazing opportunity, welcoming me into the *Life with Lucy* family. I thought that the sandwich was a nice gesture.

Gary was consistently nice to me and my friends who came around the set. Every time I would bring a female friend to the studio, he would say, "Oh, and this must be the new Mrs. Stern! Sorry I missed the wedding."

He loved to joke around.

*   *   *

Most days on the set of *Life with Lucy* were good ones, full of productivity and teamwork and light banter. However, some days were not so good. In fact, one day in particular was downright terrifying. I witnessed something that truly scared me.

On this day, Lucy was in the middle of rehearsing a scene. Things were going smoothly until all of a sudden, Lucy started to hyperventilate. Bursts of air shot through her mouth. Redness found its way onto her face. The vitality in her eyes dissolved, leaving a dullness in its wake.

Lucy started to run around the stage as if she were a helium balloon that had just lost all its air.

Panic found its way into every part of my body. I wanted to do something, but what?

Everyone else on the set started freaking out as well.

Everyone except for Gary, who took complete control of the situation.

"Don't worry about it, folks. It happens to her from time to time. Just let her go, and she'll be fine."

Within seconds, Lucy had settled down, and the color on her face was slowly coming back.

What a relief.

We all needed some air after witnessing that episode. I thought Lucy was going to die right in front of me. It was one scary afternoon.

Looking back, I'm surprised that this only happened to Lucy once during the season. She was taking on so much, working so hard, giving each and every episode her all. Most people below the age of seventy-five wouldn't last a minute with the workload that she had gladly welcomed.

When the evenings approached on the *Life with Lucy* set and it was time to go home, Lucy would always enjoy a drink. Although I had seen her perform this ritual many times, I had no idea her drink had alcohol in it. I, being the naïve young man that I was, thought it was just a slushy for her ride home.

Well, one evening, I watched Tom make her favorite "slushy." And I found out that her drink of choice was a margarita. I think she really needed it, in order to relax. Especially after the long and crazy days she was pulling.

Through the years, people have asked me, "Was Lucy a drunk? Did she drink all the time?"

The answer I always give them is that I never saw her drunk; but yes, she had a drink or two.

I think that she knew how to handle her alcohol. She was from the golden age of Hollywood, when it was glamorous for stars to drink and smoke. And Lucy could keep up with any of them.

Frank Sinatra and Clark Gable didn't have anything on her!

*   *   *

During the second week of taping, Lucy really started showing the signs of exhaustion. She had been working nonstop for a few months before the taping, preparing for the show. Now she was on the verge of burnout.

But despite all this, Lucy was intent upon plowing through. She loved working with animals, and during this week, there was going to be a real goose on the set. In the past, Lucy had worked with elephants, chimpanzees, goats, and other kinds of animals, so everyone thought that things would go smoothly with the goose.

We all thought wrong.

Right from the very first instant that the goose arrived on the set, we knew this wasn't going to be a walk in the park.

Put simply, the goose just didn't want to take his cues. He had no interest in doing what he was supposed to do. Perhaps the goose was not aware that he was working with the famous Lucille Ball. Otherwise, he would've had his act together!

Whatever the reason was, it didn't matter.

Lucy was flat-out annoyed, agitated, and worn out. The goose was not cooperating at all, and after struggling with the animal for hours, Lucy decided that she would not cooperate either. At one point, she refused to change into her wardrobe, insisting that she would wear what she was wearing—her rehearsal clothing.

The week got so tense that Gary turned and said to me, "We're going to air this show opposite World War Three."

The fact of the matter was, Lucy was working way too hard. She was cramming way too much into a four-day workweek. She desperately needed time off to recoup.

We had one more week of taping before her first week off.

Could she handle it?, I wondered.

I was worried about her, but I knew that Lucy always pulled through, no matter what the situation.

Good thing the next week had nothing to do with animals. John Ritter was set to guest star, and my guess was, he was probably going to handle his cues a lot better than that goose!

In the land of television, you can make just about anything work. And if somehow you can't, all you have to do is cut it out.

And so, in the end, the goose show never did air. It was swiftly cut from the lineup of episodes.

*   *   *

The following week when I arrived on the set, I braced myself, hoping that Lucy had recovered from the goose.

Well, sure enough, she had. I walked in, and the familiar sound of deep, husky laughter met my ears. It was Lucy, laughing like crazy. John Ritter was sitting beside her, making one joke after another. Hearing her laughter, a wave of sweet relief flooded over me.

That laughter would continue all week. It must be true what they say about laughter being the best medicine, because Lucy was back on track.

During the actual taping, Lucy was laughing so hard that she had to call out, "Cut!"

Trying to hold back her laughter, she apologized to the audience …

"This is maybe only the third time in my life that I had to stop taping because of my laughing!"

John just had a way with humor. He could bring Lucy to pieces with his fearless wit and sharp comedic timing. John carried a joy within him that was utterly contagious. That week, through all kinds of giggles, Lucy kept saying that she had Ritter-itus.

About a month later, I was at a Sherman Oaks newsstand, looking for magazines that had stories with Lucy in them. Around that time, the John Ritter episode was about to air.

Oddly enough, I noticed a guy behind me who was picking up all the same magazines that I was looking at. He was wearing a baseball cap and dark sunglasses. I squinted my eyes and studied him closely before I realized that it was John Ritter.

He was also collecting stories about Lucy.

I reintroduced myself to him. We talked about that week.

"It was so special to have that whole week with her," John said.

He told me that he had learned so much from Lucy. A few weeks after taping with us, he had done the *Bill Cosby Show*. He marveled at the fact that he had worked with two of the funniest people in the world and that they both had different approaches to getting to the end result. Lucy liked to rehearse over and over again to achieve near-perfect cohesion; Bill would rehearse just once or twice. John told me that he was more like Lucy and preferred to rehearse a scene over and over again as well.

It was nice to hear that John had such a great experience on the set. Little did he know that his presence was a much-needed antidote for Lucy's spirit, giving her just the boost she needed to press on.

CHAPTER 38

During one of our lunch breaks, Lucy, Tom, and I were in the dressing room. I was discussing the different shows that I had been watching on television over the last few days. I brought up one of the story lines, which was about a couple who had marital problems. In it, the man kept cheating on his wife.

The whole time I noticed that Tom was giving me the evil eye. It was almost as if he was telling me to please shut my mouth. I realized that I was teetering too close to the brink of an uncomfortable place: the subject of Lucy and Desi's relationship.

Instantly, I sped toward another topic of conversation: Patty Duke.

Patty Duke is, to me, one of the few actresses who can fully embody the world of the character that she's portraying. She becomes the character, completing transforming herself into another person. Her talent is immense, and my respect for her has always been high.

"She's one of the best actresses around," I told Lucy, eager to stop Tom from continuing his evil-eye routine.

But that didn't help. In fact, Tom still kept giving me the evil eye. And beyond that, he was also starting to kick me under the table.

What was going on? I scanned the insides of my brain, trying to figure out what I was saying wrong this time.

Wait …

Could it have been the fact that I was telling one of the most famous actresses around that I thought Patty Duke was the best actress?

Ooops.

I hadn't meant to bring Lucy down in any way. My love of her talent was beyond common knowledge at that point. Surely she wasn't hurt by that comment about another actress.

And before I could question the situation any further, Lucy's next words cleared the mystery right up for me.

"Patty Duke is a wonderful actress," she said. "And, you know, Patty and Desi dated for a while."

In an instant, it all made sense.

I looked over at Tom, who wore a coat of disappointment on his face. I had completely forgotten that Desi Jr. and Patty had a romance years earlier, and it was known that Lucy wasn't too crazy about the relationship at first. The thing was, I never worried about editing myself while talking to Lucy. My level of comfort with her was strong, and I wasn't concerned about choosing my words carefully or presenting myself a certain way.

Never did it cross my mind to censor myself.

In 2002, the chance to meet Patty Duke fell right into my lap. She was doing a play in Los Angeles called *Follies*. Wanda and I went to see our good friend Carole Cook, who was also appearing in the play. I relished every opportunity to watch Carole on stage. She was larger than life, always able to completely take over the stage with her tremendous presence. Carole is so right at home in front of a big audience. It's a delight to watch her at work. Carole was Lucy's protégé, going back to the late fifties. They became so close that Lucy was Carole's maid of honor at her wedding.

After *Follies* was finished, the all-star cast went outside to the portable dressing rooms and met with family and friends. There I saw Patty speaking to a couple of people, so I waited for a free moment to talk to her.

Within minutes, I was standing right next to Patty, telling her how wonderful a performer she was, telling her that I had raved about her acting in front of Lucy.

Patty responded by saying great things about Lucy. She told me that early on, they never saw eye to eye; but over the years, they did become very friendly with one another.

We ended up speaking for about ten minutes. Sometimes you meet celebrities and find that they're not what you expected them to be. However, with Patty Duke, it was just the opposite. She was just like the person who I had always envisioned she was—sweet, generous, and patient. Her immense talent was not her only attribute. She was absolutely wonderful.

CHAPTER 39

While filming *Life with Lucy*, Lucy got invited to appear on the new FOX network talk show, *The Late Show*, hosted by Joan Rivers. The theme of the night was first ladies. Nancy Reagan, the sitting First Lady of the United States, was going to be on the show. Lucy was invited as the first lady of television, and Michelle Lee was invited as the first lady of the prime-time soap *Knot's Landing*.

It was October 30, 1986. Since Nancy Reagan was going to be in the building, a major security search was required for all who entered the studio. After undergoing my search, I arrived at the stage door and was sent to Lucy's dressing room, where I waited for her to arrive.

She got there a few minutes later, looking spectacular in a purple pantsuit and purple shoes that I had sold to her from the department store. Lucy was accompanied by Paula Stewart and Tom Watson.

The dressing room was one of the largest I had ever seen. An overflowing spread of food sat on a few tables along the walls. There were finger sandwiches, fine wines, cheeses, vegetables, and little cakes.

About twenty minutes before the show was to begin, there was a knock on the door. It was the Secret Service. In a firm tone, one of the men told us all to stay in the room and not to move, as the first lady was coming in the building.

At that moment, things became really exciting. The four of us did as we were told. We stayed in the room and remained still, not making a sound.

About five minutes later, there was another knock on the door. This time it was a young lady. She introduced herself, saying she was from Nancy Reagan's camp.

"Miss Ball, Mrs. Reagan would like to see you now," the young lady said politely, clearing enunciating each word.

And so Lucy said, as only Lucy could, "Okay, please send Mrs. Reagan in now."

The young lady's face dropped all the way to the floor. She stood there, no words coming to her lips. In her head, she must have been thinking: *How do you tell Lucille Ball that she is the one who has to go over to see the first lady?*

Lucy let the young lady off the hook with a smile. She had only been joking. Of course, she would go over and see the first lady. How do you turn down an invitation like that? Lucy and Mrs. Reagan had been friends for many years.

All of us headed over to meet Mrs. Reagan, and Lucy introduced me, Tom, and Paula. A very tiny lady, Mrs. Reagan was extremely sweet and good-natured. I liked her personality right away.

Later on, in discussing the first lady's size, Lucy said, "It was like hugging a toothpick."

When we got back to her dressing room, Lucy became immediately upset. She felt that she wasn't dressed appropriately for the show. I thought that Lucy looked particularly amazing that night. But all the other ladies were wearing black formal outfits.

After Mrs. Reagan's interview was completed, Lucy was up. It was her time to shine, once again. She started to talk about *Life with Lucy* and how upset she was about the negative reviews.

"Some of the reviewers said that I should be dead," Lucy told Joan, her voice full of disbelief.

Lucy went on to say that she would not have minded criticisms about the show or her performance, but that mean insults about her age or how she looked really hurt her.

"Tell them to pick a finger!" Joan exclaimed, rallying to Lucy's side.

A wide smile found its way onto Lucy's face.

She got the joke.

CHAPTER 40

One afternoon I was walking Lucy to her dressing room on the other side of the lot when I noticed two young men waiting around. I could smell their motives from yards away. They wanted Lucy's autograph. Being an avid autograph collector myself, I could just see it in the way they were standing there, waiting.

And I was right.

The two young men wasted no time approaching Lucy and telling her what big fans they were and how they were looking forward to *Life with Lucy*. Lucy signed an autograph for each of them and disappeared into her dressing room. Seconds later she stuck her head out of her dressing room, beckoning for the guys to return.

"I want you two to know that *Life with Lucy* will air on ABC, channel 7, at 8:00 p.m. Saturday nights. Please watch," Lucy told the guys.

They both nodded profusely, telling her that they would definitely be watching.

If Lucy had had the time, she probably would have gone door to door, just to let everyone know. The fact that she was a major celebrity did not mean that she wanted to cut herself off from the outside world. In fact, it was just the opposite. Lucy wanted nothing more than to be a normal, real person.

One day in her dressing room, she noticed a stain on the carpet.

"Let me call housekeeping, and they'll remove it," I assured her.

"Nonsense!" Lucy replied.

She went off to her kitchen and found a bottle of cleaner. Then she got on her hands and knees to get to work and clean the spot. She always knew how to keep it real.

Just like the time she went to a taping of *The Merv Griffin Show*. Lucy had invited me to attend with her, so I showed up at the studio, positioning myself by the stage door, waiting for Lucy to arrive.

Minutes later I spotted Lucy pulling into the studio lot. To my surprise, she was in the driver's seat of the car. This was the only time that I had ever seen Lucy drive herself to a television event without someone like Howard McClay, Frank Gorey, Tom Watson, or Gary escorting her. I guess there's a first time for everything.

One of the valet attendants plucked open Lucy's door, and she stepped out of her car, looking like the major television star that she was. Her eyes scanned the eager crowd of forty people who were standing out front, waiting for the chance to ask for her autograph. Then she spotted me and quickly said, "Michael, come with me. I'm late."

Before I had a chance to reply, she grabbed my arm. "I'm late, very late. Please hurry with me inside."

With that, we whizzed by the crowd and stepped into the studio. Since she was in such a hurry, she didn't have the time to sign a single autograph, which was very unusual for her. Lucy was always up for signing autographs when the time permitted.

As soon as we were out of earshot from the folks outside, Lucy sighed and said, "I am sooo early."

I realized that she had purposely gotten herself out of signing autographs. She knew that if she signed for one person, she would have to sign for everyone. Not only did Lucy keep it real, but she *always* wanted things to be fair.

On another visit to *The Merv Griffin Show*, we were in a large green room, which was full of food and drinks. Lucy was waiting to be called to the stage.

A young man approached Lucy with an 8 x 10 photo of her. The photo had been taken by paparazzi and sold to him on Hollywood Boulevard. It wasn't the most flattering picture of Lucy. Anyone could have seen that from a mile away.

"Would you sign this for me?" the man asked politely, holding the picture up in front of Lucy.

She gave him a smile and signed the photo.

A few minutes went by.

Lucy went over to the gentleman and asked, "Can I have the picture back?"

Although he was a bit surprised, the man responded, "Yes."

Lucy then explained that the picture was just awful, not in the least bit flattering. She told him that she would send him another autographed picture in the mail.

And so the very next day, Lucy signed a photo for the guy and sent it out to him. Always true to her word, Lucy was someone who loved being in touch with the people. There was no question about it.

CHAPTER 41

There were four directors on *Life with Lucy*. Each one was assigned to do about four shows each. No one ever told me why that was, but I'm sure it was so they could pick just one or two of them to do the rest of the season.

One of the directors was a man named Bruce Bilson. During his long career, he had done such shows as *Get Smart* and *M*A*S*H*. I remember after lunch one day, we were about to resume rehearsals, and everyone was still chatting among themselves. Frustrated, Bruce leaned toward the cast and crew.

"I don't care what *you* had for lunch, or what *you* had for lunch, or what *you* had for lunch," Bruce yelled, pointing his finger at random people in the studio. "I just want this set quiet!"

After he was through screaming, silence greeted him. Everyone sat there, mouths shut, afraid of making another peep.

But then about fifteen seconds later, Lucy opened her mouth and cried out, "I had salmon!"

Laughter burst out from every direction.

The set turned back to normal.

Lucy always knew how to gain control of the environment. She always knew how to steer a tense and frustrated set back to a happy set. Each and every day, that was what she aimed for. As a crew and cast, we had such a blast working with one another.

One week during some downtime, we were all playing Password. Lucy was set to appear on the game show with Ann Dusenberry in the coming weeks. In order to prepare her for it, we spent every break shouting out words to see if Lucy would get them right. We even took the time to set up the back of the stage as a mini *Password* set.

Not only did we know how to work hard, but we knew how to have a lively time doing it!

*   *   *

One of my favorite episodes of *Life with Lucy* was when actress Audrey Meadows came on for a week. She was also from the golden age of television, having worked with "The Great One," Jackie Gleason, on the *Honeymooners*.

It was a wonderful experience, watching two ol' pros working together. The mastery, the skill, and the sharpness on display was mind-blowing. They both respected each other's work, and that made them more of a pleasure to watch. Their chemistry together was beautiful. It was the first time during the *Life with Lucy* shows that Lucy was working with another female her own age. It was just like watching Lucy and Ethel. The nostalgia came back full force, and as I watched Lucy and Audrey, I thought to myself: *Savor this moment.*

During the final dress rehearsal, Audrey, who was playing Lucy's sister, already had her stage makeup put on. The thing was, the scene they were acting out required Lucy to smear Audrey's face with food.

Lucy didn't realize until after the food fight that Audrey had to go back and have her makeup applied again. She felt horrible for Audrey and kept apologizing to her for the oversight.

"It's okay," Audrey kept telling Lucy, trying to put her at ease.

Despite Audrey's claim that everything was fine, Lucy still felt bad.

Watching these two women work was such a treat. Audrey was asked to come back for more shows, which would have been terrific. The show definitely benefited from her presence. Her chemistry with Lucy was truly something worth watching.

It's too bad that we didn't get Audrey on earlier episodes of the show. Things might have turned out differently.

*   *   *

Although Lucy thought that the show *Laverne and Shirley* was covering the same ground that Lucy and Ethel had years earlier, she still loved to watch it. She also mentioned how much she liked the show *Perfect Strangers*.

"That's my type of comedy," she told me one day.

I ended up attending a taping of *Perfect Strangers* and was fortunate enough to meet Bronson Pinchot after the show. We talked for about fifteen minutes, and I told him all about how I was working with Lucy. Hearing this, he was inspired to write a fan letter to Lucy on the back page of his script. He wrote that he really admired her and hoped to meet her one day.

After seeing what he had written, I looked up at him. "I could arrange that."

I invited him and his costar, Mark Linn-Baker, to come to an upcoming taping of *Life with Lucy*. We exchanged phone numbers and set it up within days.

We didn't know it at the time, but Bronson and Mark would be attending what was to be the last taping of *Life with Lucy*.

The day was November 6, 1986. The guys arrived early, and I went to get them at the gate. After hopping into Bronson's car, we drove over to the soundstage.

Since Lucy was getting her makeup done, I couldn't take them to see her right away. The show was going to be starting soon, and I knew that Lucy needed time alone to prepare. So I escorted Bronson and Mark to their seats. Minutes later, the show began.

During Gary's warm-up, he introduced Bronson and Mark, and they spoke to the audience. Everyone there was delighted to see them, as *Perfect Strangers* was a major television hit at the time. A feeling of pride danced in my chest. It felt good to know that I was the one responsible for them being there on that day.

After the show, I brought Bronson and Mark down to the set. When Lucy laid eyes on them, it was as if a shot of oxygen had been released into her system. She became instantly animated, just as a fan would be in the presence of an idol.

"I love your show!" she declared. "I watch it all the time. You're both very good!"

She gushed over them, and they gushed right back over her.

A friend of mine named Rick Carl was an audience member who attended every show. He is a very talented artist and one of the founding members of the We Love Lucy fan club. After the first *Life with Lucy* show he presented Lucy with a special caricature to welcome her back to series television. She enjoyed the artwork so much that she had it hanging in her home.

Rick was smart to have his camera on hand during the series, and on this night he took many great photos of Lucy with Bronson and Mark.

I saw Bronson a few times after that day, as I attended some other *Perfect Strangers* tapings. He confided in me that meeting Lucy had changed his attitude about fans.

"Now I take more time meeting my fans. I don't take them for granted any longer."

Bronson had always been friendly to his fans, but now he was also going to be sure to appreciate them more.

During that *Life with Lucy* taping, Gary was the only one who knew the show had been canceled. He was informed of the bad news that afternoon and didn't say a word to anyone. I think he didn't want the news to affect anyone's performance that night.

After that taping, *Life with Lucy* would no longer be in production. I heard that during Lucy's ride home, Gary broke the news to her: She had been *fired*.

*   *   *

I was back at my desk on Friday, working at Robinson's, when Tom called and told me the news. Feeling as if I had been crushed by a two-ton weight, there was no way I was going to be able to focus at my job for the rest of the day. I left and drove over to Warner Hollywood Studios, where I was told to go right into Gary's office. When I got there, I found Tom and Gary talking.

Gary turned to look at me, and the first thing he said was, "Aren't you glad you didn't quit your day job?"

Within a couple of hours, everyone had gathered over at the studio; we were all shocked by the news. A small impromptu get-together was under way at Bob and Madelyn's office. On one table, there were food and drinks, and on another table, prop items from the set, free for the taking. Wanting to grab a memento of the entire experience, I took a tube of Wacky Glue from the episode "Lucy Gets Her Wires Crossed"

Everyone from the cast and crew was there, except for Larry Anderson, who was auditioning to be a host for a new version of *Truth or Consequences*. Lucky for him, he got the gig. (And thanks to Larry, I also later got a new part-time gig on the game show.)

But back to that day ...

Always one who looked at the brighter side of things, Lucy joked around with everybody, trying to be uplifting and positive. She felt bad for the crew, as she thought they would be out of jobs for the season.

She took the two young people who had played her grandkids, Jenny Lewis and Philip J. Amelio II, to a corner of the office and sat down with each of them privately. She wanted them to know that this was not the end of their careers, that this turn of events had nothing to do with them. Lucy had taken on the persona of a kind and generous grandmother, who wanted the best for everyone.

When only Gale, Tom, and I were within earshot, she said to us, "You know, I've never been fired before."

But there was no sadness beneath the words. Lucy took it all with a grain of salt, believing she would find other projects to do. Life goes on!

I studied Lucy carefully, amazed by all the strength that she was exhibiting.

Her comforting words really inspired the group to look toward the future with hope.

About an hour later, as I walked Lucy out to her dressing room, something unexpected happened.

She broke down and started to cry.

"I've just lost all of my friends, and now I'll never work in the business again," she wailed as tears slid down her cheeks.

"That's not true," I said to Lucy, trying to comfort her, trying to be as strong as she had been back in the office. "You'll be back. The whole world loves you. Trust me, they do."

Gratitude found its way into Lucy's eyes. "Thank God, I still have *you*."

With that, Lucy wiped her tears away. She took a breath, collected herself, and kept on moving.

Although the television world had rejected her, she was going to press on.

Lucy had never been one to allow obstacles to get the best of her. It was good to see that even after she had gotten fired for the first time nothing had changed.

*   *   *

I took another souvenir that day: Lucy's parking-spot tag.

Lucy had the best parking spot on the lot, and over the course of the show's tapings, I was able to use her spot quite often. It was in front of her main dressing room on the lot.

On that last day, I parked in the spot and took the sign. About three hours later, I had to drive off the lot for a few minutes to run an errand. When I returned, I found that someone was in the spot.

I went over to the guard gate and told the guards that someone was in Lucy's spot. I also brought to their attention the fact that the signage was missing.

One of the guards shook his head and chuckled. "Those fans will take anything."

"I know!" I replied, glad that I had covered my tracks.

It was a good thing the guard never checked my trunk!

Backstage pictures at Life with Lucy *with Bronson Pinchot and Mark Linn-Baker (Photo by Rick Carl)*

Lucy and Gary with Bronson Pinchot and Mark Linn-Baker (Photo by Rick Carl)

With John Ritter (Photo by Rick Carl)

With Kenny Rogers (Photo by Rick Carl)

*With Gale Gordon and Lucy, the day I found
out* Life with Lucy *was canceled.*

CHAPTER 42

A few weeks later, Ann Dusenberry and Larry Anderson threw a barbeque wrap party for the cast and crew (at a house rented by the family of Jenny Lewis) in the San Fernando Valley. All of us showed up in good spirits, radiating positive attitudes.

Looking around at everyone who I had worked with for all those weeks, I realized that we had all become very close. As Lucy always strived to make the set a drama-free zone, our relationships were easy and not full of conflict. We had become a tight-knit family.

Lucy and Gary arrived at the party with their little dog, Tinker. After saying hello to everyone, Lucy headed for the backyard and parked herself in a chair. All day people kept approaching her to chat and take pictures.

When Gale arrived with his wife, Lucy gave him an early Christmas gift—a VCR.

The party lasted for hours. When it was finally over, we looked around and saw that there was still a lot of food out on the tables. Ann enlisted my help, and we drove to downtown Los Angeles, dropping the leftovers off at a food pantry for the homeless.

Lucy with Tinker

*   *   *

A couple of weeks later, Lucy taped a week's worth of *Super Password* episodes. On the show, Betty White and Estelle

182

Getty were a team, while Lucy was paired up with Ann Dusenberry. It was *The Golden Girls* versus *Life with Lucy*.

On the day of the first taping, Tom and I both drove separately to the NBC Studios in Burbank. We met Lucy, who arrived by limo, backstage. It was so refreshing to see her back at a studio.

However, Lucy was not in the best of moods. She was still feeling the hurt of the *Life with Lucy* cancellation.

And there was also something else. Desi Sr. was ill, and she knew he did not have much time.

Lucy had a lot rolling around in her mind. But upon entering the studio, she did her best to push everything aside. She had to become "Lucille Ball." She pushed all her worries delicately aside, knowing that she could come back to them after the taping.

Wanting to make sure she was okay, Tom offered to sit with Lucy during her ride home in the limo.

"I can follow the limo and then drive you back to the studio to pick up your car," I offered.

After the show was finished for the day, we caravanned over to Lucy's house. When we got there, she must have been exhausted, as she went right upstairs to her bedroom. Now that she was away from the studio, she was left to face the worries that she had pushed out of her mind earlier in the day. In other words, she needed her privacy.

*   *   *

A few weeks later, on December 2, Desi Sr. passed away in Del Mar, California. Lucie was at his bedside.

Since I had only met Desi a couple of times, I can't say that he was a friend of mine. But each time I had the pleasure of speaking with the man, I was absolutely floored by the kindness that was gushing out of him. I also felt that he knew I was more than just an average fan.

Desi's memorial was quite lovely. It was a full house, packed with all the people who loved him. The event was held in Del Mar, about one hundred miles from Los Angeles, right near San Diego.

I drove down with my friend Valerie. When we got there, we found Lucy and Gary already present. I had assumed that the whole Hollywood community would be there, as Desi was quite a fixture in the entertainment world. With the loads of dedication and talent he had applied to his work, he really molded the world of television.

But the only two celebrities in attendance were Dean Paul Martin—the son of Dean Martin, and one third of the group Dino, Desi, and Billy—and comedian/actor Danny Thomas, who spoke.

Before the service, Lucie thanked me for attending. "It's nice that you're here on behalf of his many fans," she said, moisture in her beautiful eyes.

Lucie spoke at the service as well, reading from her father's book, *A Book*. She then thanked all the nurses and his horse-racing friends who were present. After the service ended, we were all invited to Desi Sr.'s house for lunch.

Hearts were broken on that day, but one thing was for certain—Desi Arnaz's amazing legacy would live on for many years to come.

Days after Desi's passing, a news reporter stuck a microphone in Lucy's face, asking her, "What does the death of Desi mean to you?"

Without pausing for a moment, Lucy spoke about what a great man Desi was. She talked about what an amazing father he was. How he had done so much for the television industry. How he had been a great innovator and businessman. She respected him immensely, and his passing really broke her heart.

However, as Lucy always had a way of maintaining her strength, she showed up at all her public appearances, with a smile on her face.

While she was taping *Life with Lucy*, Lucy had got word that she had been nominated for the prestigious Kennedy Center Honors Award by one of her old friends, Danny Kaye, and had soon been chosen to be an honoree.

Kennedy Center Honors was one of the last major awards that Lucy would receive while she was alive.

After all the negative reviews had come out for her canceled show, Lucy said, "I better accept this award because it will be the last award that anyone would want to give me."

The show was filmed in Washington DC, just a few days after Desi's service. Lucy's tribute had to be rewritten, because of Lucie and Desi Jr. canceling their appearances at the last minute. And so the new Lucy tribute host was Robert Stack. Lucy's costars Bea Arthur from *Mame* and Valerie Harper from *Wildcat* were also there. Pam Dawber, from the series *Mork and Mindy*, even sang a tribute song to Lucy.

During the show, one could easily tell by the emotion on Lucy's face that she was deeply touched. Watching her, the world also felt a tinge of sadness, as everyone was highly aware of Desi's passing.

When Lucy came back to California, she was so proud of the award and took every opportunity to show it off. To me, she almost seemed like a little kid who had won a first-prize ribbon at the fair.

CHAPTER 43

One day while working at Robinson's, I received a phone call from Lucy.

"It's time to get more sheets for my bed," she announced.

"We have a great sale on white sheets that are irregulars. They might have a flaw or two in them, though."

"That's fine," Lucy assured me. "I need ten sets."

As I always loved to be of service to Lucy, a jolt of energy filled my body and made me stand a little straighter. I had another mission!

"I'll mail them out to you today," I told Lucy before we hung up from one another.

I zipped through the store and went right to work, targeting all the bottom and top sheets I could find. In the end, I only came across ten bottom ones and six top ones.

Figuring it would be okay, I went ahead and mailed them out.

Big mistake.

A couple of days later, I received another call from Lucy. This time, she was irate. This was a side of her that I had never seen or heard before.

"How dare you only give me ten bottom sheets and six top sheets!" Lucy exclaimed. "The sets are not equal now!"

Her anger was epic. I reached inside myself for a way to respond to her, to bring her to a normal state.

"Lucy, it's okay. I'll be able to get another four top sheets in a few days."

I held my breath, waiting for her response. Instead of more words, Lucy simply hung the phone up on me.

I stared at the receiver in my hand. *Was what I had done really worth all the frustration? Was our friendship, after all those years, over?* My heart sank into my chest.

Not knowing what to do, I called Wanda right away.

No sooner had she finished saying hello than I spat out, "Wanda, Lucy yelled at me."

I explained to Wanda what had happened. After listening to the whole story, Wanda tried to assure me that everything was fine. "You know, Michael, that means that Lucy loves you. She would only be real to those who know her."

After hearing Wanda's explanation, I felt somewhat better. Once I got off the phone with her, I threw myself into high gear. For the next few hours, I called every Robinson's in the state. After being placed on hold many times, I was able to track down some top sheets. I had them mailed to her right away.

Wanting to give Lucy a heads-up, I called her home. Frank answered the phone.

"Can you tell Lucy that I was able to get her the remaining top sheets, and that she should expect them in the next couple of days?"

"I'll let Lucy know," Frank answered in his affable way.

Days went by before Lucy finally called me. She told me that the sheets had arrived. She also went on to explain that Choo Choo (the maid) changed the sheets every day, and that she liked working with matching sets that were, of course, even. Lucy said nothing about losing her temper the other week. It was as if it never happened.

But I didn't mind that. I had found my way back into her good graces, and that was all that mattered.

*   *   *

One morning I was awakened by the ringing telephone on my nightstand. Through half-closed eyes, I looked over at the clock. It was 5:30 a.m. Groaning, I reached for the phone and pressed it against my ear.

It was Lucy.

"Michael, I hope I didn't wake you up, but I've been thinking about Desi's apartment."

She was helping Desi Jr. redecorate his house, and needed me to pick up a comforter set with pillows and sheets.

My body pinned to the bed and my eyes still heavy with sleep, I told her, "I'll look around."

"Desi's going to call you."

About fifteen minutes later, at around 5:45 a.m., the phone rang yet again. It was Desi. His voice on the other end sounded tired and low.

"Did your mom wake you up too?" I asked him.

"Yes!" he responded.

Apparently, Lucy had become inspired and wanted to work on the redecorating *right now*.

After Desi gave me more of a sense of what he wanted, I told him I would look around and call him in the afternoon. As we hung up, I shook my head, thinking about Lucy's urge to get the redecorating process under way. I just hoped it wasn't like episode 74 in *I Love Lucy* when Lucy tries to redecorate the Mertzes' apartment! (Needless to say, things don't go exactly as planned in that episode.)

Later that day, I found something that I thought Desi would like, and Frank came by the store to pick everything up.

A couple of hours after that, Lucy called. "You did really well. Keep looking for those sales for me."

Within a year I had moved from the linen department to the women's shoe department. This was a huge deal for me, a promotion of sorts. Now I would start receiving 9 percent commission. There was an opportunity to make more than I ever had before.

I told Lucy about the move, and she was so happy for me. One of her favorite brands of shoes was Bruno Magli. At that time the shoes were selling for almost two hundred dollars a pair. She told me that she was a size seven and a half, and that she liked a short heel with an open toe. Lucy had Wanda open a credit card with both my name and Lucy's name on it. That way I was able to sell shoes to her without her having to come down to the store. I would sell her about ten to twelve pairs of shoes at a time and then deliver them to her home. She would usually keep all of them, except for maybe a pair or two.

One day, while she was trying on the shoes at her home, she told me, "We have to do this fast."

"Why?"

"Gary's sister, Helen, is coming over, and if she sees these shoes, she'd want to keep them all for herself."

I loved it when she appeared on shows and specials, because I always got to brag to anyone in sight, "I sold her those shoes."

Years later, after Lucy had passed away, I was helping Lucie go through her things. We found a number of unused shoes. After seeing that, I wondered if she had only bought them to guide my sales upward.

After being in the women's shoe department for some time, my next move was to the furniture and mattress department. While I was there, Lucy bought about ten sets of mattresses from me. Talk about commission! She helped me make my quota often, purchasing mattresses for her Beverly Hills house, her Palm Springs house, and Desi's house.

Whenever Lucy needed a last-minute gift—which was often—she called me at work.

It was always "Mike, dear, could you please pick up a man's sweater for me? It's Stuart's birthday." Or "Mike, dear, Gary needs more towels for his bathroom."

She loved it whenever I was able to get her my employee discount.

A penny saved is a penny earned. And everybody wants a good price, no matter how much money he or she has.

CHAPTER 44

Almost one year to the day that *Life with Lucy* was announced, we were back at the Museum of Broadcasting's annual event. Each year the museum would honor about ten shows or performers from television, either past or present. Lucy had agreed to do her Q&A for the big event.

It was March 2, 1987. In my usual fashion, I set about procuring autographs from the myriad of celebrities who filled the museum. Working the room that night, I must have received about ten autographs. Sometimes I would ask a person for an autograph, even though I had gotten it in the past. That night I got autographs from people like Sid Caesar, Julie Andrews, Milton Berle, Bob Hope, and Joyce Randolph from *The Honeymooners*.

Later in the evening, I spotted Victoria Principal, who was starring in *Dallas*, my favorite show at the time. I, along with everyone else who wasn't living under a rock, had recently heard that she was about to leave the series. This big news was circulating the globe, and everyone was talking about Victoria Principal.

Seeing my opportunity, I walked up to her. "Can I please have your autograph?"

"No," Victoria responded firmly. "If I sign for you, I would have to sign for everyone in here."

I looked around at the star-studded room and then back at Victoria. "But I'm the only person asking for autographs."

Tired of me, Victoria all but rolled her eyes. "I'll shake your hand," she offered, her voice flat.

Here was someone whom I truly admired, and she was coldly saying no to signing an autograph. I could understand if she was eating at a restaurant or out with her family, but she was at a *celebrity event*. One thing I learned early on was that there was a good time to ask for an autograph, as well as a bad time. This setting seemed like the perfect place. I was utterly confused by her refusal.

I went over to Lucy and said, "Victoria Principal wouldn't sign an autograph for me."

A displeased look on her face, Lucy stabbed her eyes across the room at Victoria, who didn't notice what was going on.

"Then you don't want it," Lucy muttered.

Lucy knew how important fans were to the whole equation, and she wasn't crazy about celebrities who had no respect for the people who loved them. If a celebrity didn't have any fans, where would he/she be?

That night I escorted Lucy to her car and noticed—who else?—Victoria Principal standing outside.

Victoria's entire face lit up when she laid eyes on Lucy. "Hello, Lucy, how are you? Sorry that I missed you inside."

Lucy barely glanced at Victoria and said, "Hi … Oh, here's my car. I have to go." She turned toward me with warm eyes. "Bye, Michael. I'll see you soon."

And within seconds, Lucy disappeared into her car.

And there I was. Standing next to Victoria Principal. Alone.

After a moment of awkward silence, Victoria said to me, "I can sign that autograph now."

Although the voice inside told me to hold my ground and refuse it, I couldn't bring myself to say no to an autograph! I eagerly pulled out the pad for Victoria to sign. There was no denying that celebrities and their autographs were my biggest weaknesses.

Two days later, it was time for Lucy's Q&A. But before the show began, she was informed that she would be doing a television interview via satellite with Bob Osborne, her long-time Desilu workshop student for the CBS morning news.

Panic pumped through Lucy's insides. She hadn't been notified of the interview earlier and only had her street makeup on. She told me that she needed false eyelashes.

"There's a May Company down the street. I'll run and get you a pair," I told Lucy, right before I bolted out of the museum.

After zipping down Wilshire Boulevard, I made it to the May Company, which was about five blocks down. Out of breath, I pushed the door open and slipped inside the store.

A girl behind the counter saw me come in, and she must have thought I was prepared to rob the place, because she called security.

Couldn't she see that all I wanted was a pair of eyelashes?

Well, security approached me, and I explained my situation. They told me that May Company didn't sell eyelashes. Defeated, I headed out of the store and raced back to the museum.

Out of breath once again, I went inside and informed Lucy that May Company didn't sell the lashes.

Unwilling to give up the mission, I enlisted the help of my friend Richard Brock, who was backstage with us. We both hopped into his car and drove down various streets, peering out of the window, looking for any sign of a drugstore.

Then we finally spotted one.

After parking, we ran into the store, our bodies alert and our eyes wide open. We were two guys looking for eyelashes.

When we found them, we both stood there staring, almost paralyzed. There were so many options: long lashes, short lashes, brown lashes, black lashes, curly lashes. What to choose?

A lady working there asked us what size we were looking for.

Eyelashes had sizes? It was the first I had heard of it.

Richard and I ended up buying about ten pairs. Now we just had to get them back to her, and the mission would truly be accomplished.

When we got back to the museum, we discovered that Lucy had already done the interview. We were too late. Not wanting to feel that I had wasted my time, I tried to look on the bright side; I had learned a lesson. Now if anyone ever asks me to pick up a pair of eyelashes, I will know where to get them and to inquire about what size he or she needs beforehand. (Not like anyone has ever asked me to run an errand like that again in the twenty-plus years since!)

About ten minutes later, we walked Lucy to the stage. We went the back way, traipsing through hallways and traveling down employee elevators.

As we neared the stage, Lucy angled her body toward me. "You know, Cary Grant died this way."

A chuckle escaped my lips.

Although she had said it as a joke, I think that Lucy was a bit nervous. Perhaps she thought her fans wouldn't come out to support her. She had suffered quite a blow from the cancellation of *Life with Lucy*, which had rendered her unsure of herself.

Well, if she was worried about the lack of support from her fans, she didn't have to worry any longer.

Once she stepped out onto the stage, she was greeted with an overwhelming wave of clapping and cheering—a wave that moved throughout the room with tremendous force, as if it would never stop.

CHAPTER 45

One day as I entered Lucy's house, Frank told me to take off my shoes. *This was a first.*

I looked and realized that there was new white carpeting throughout the entire house. And I don't mean *off-white*; I mean *white-white*. Lucy jokingly said it was a little too white and that she needed sunglasses the first few days to avoid blindness.

Her whole place had been redone, courtesy of Paula Stewart (Lucy's *Wildcat* costar), who had become an interior decorator.

In Lucy's lanai room, Paula redid her sofa and had a humongous coffee table brought in. From the second it arrived, Lucy started flashing dirty looks at the coffee table. She wasn't in love with it at all.

Lucy was not one who embraced change easily. Even when it came to pets, Lucy had a hard time letting go.

I remember one day when I came over, Lucy had just gotten a new dog named Tinker. This dog was replacing her other poodle, who had recently passed away, also named Tinker. Lucy told me that this new dog was Tinker #3. From his nose to his eyes to his little tail, he looked exactly like her old dog. The familiarity brought her great comfort.

I remember sitting with Lucy on the lanai room floor, playing with Tinker #3 all afternoon. We would sit and throw a ball, prompting Tinker to go and chase it.

Once, Lucy signed an autograph for me on the surface of a picture of her and Tinker. She wrote the words "For Mike, With Love, Lucy & Tinker."

Now, I wasn't sure which Tinker it was in the photo (I'm still not sure), but I didn't want to bother her by asking her. I guess it didn't matter. They all looked the same, anyhow.

CHAPTER 46

After a good, long run, I finally left Robinson's to seek out something new and different. I ended up working at a furniture store that was closer to my home. At first, it seemed to be the biggest mistake of my life. I wasn't crazy about the way they did business or the way I was being treated. I felt unappreciated and undervalued and started wondering why I had ever left Robinson's in the first place.

The furniture store was called Wickes Furniture; however, Lucy kept calling it *Mary Wickes* furniture.

Before I started the job, I went on a trip to London. This was in February of 1989. I went to visit my friend Craig, who was staying in England for six months. It was my very first time going overseas.

Before I left, Lucy said to me, "Have a good time. And don't eat fish and chips all the time! Fried food is not good for you!"

Jokingly, I asked, "You want me to say hi to the queen for you?"

"Sure," Lucy grinned. "Also, say hi to the queen's mum for me."

Craig and I were not about to waste a minute of precious time in London. For two weeks, we spent every single day sightseeing, taking in every piece of the enchanting city that we could.

In an English newspaper, I found a daily column that announced where members of the royal family would be. Some days, it would say, "No public appearances today." During the second-to-last day that I was there, it was announced that the queen was going to be at Kensington Gardens for a tree planting at 3:30 p.m. Eager to meet the queen and deliver a greeting from Lucy, I told Craig about the tree planting.

Uninterested, Craig shook his head and frowned. "I don't want to go. It's gonna be crazy over there. I don't want to spend hours and hours waiting just to get a glimpse of the queen."

"Well, I'm going!" I declared.

And so, three hours before the queen was set to appear, I arrived at the location. There was nothing set up. Puzzled, I looked around, taking everything in. There were no crowds; there wasn't even a sign that indicated that the queen would be there. For a minute, I assumed I was at the wrong place.

I went up to some of the people who worked in the gardens and asked where the queen was going to be that day. They had no clue. I decided to hang around and wait a little longer.

After an hour passed, I saw some people setting up some stanchions.

Approaching them, I asked, "Is this where the queen will be?"

"Yes," one of the guys responded.

Finally. I got the confirmation that I was looking for.

As I continued to watch the workers set everything up, something started to really perplex me. I wondered why there was no one else around but me. Where were the lines of people that Craig was so concerned about?

About thirty minutes before the queen was set to appear, a group of kids showed up on a bus. There were also some people from the gardens, who started positioning themselves toward the area that the workers had set up. One thing I didn't see, however, was security. I figured that they were acting discreet and standing by somewhere.

Finally, a polished-looking male stood in front of everyone and sternly said, "Remember: Do not touch the queen if she does come by."

And that was it. Those were the only instructions we ever received.

Right at 3:30 p.m. a car that looked like a Honda pulled up, and the queen's Rolls Royce pulled up right behind it. The queen exited the car, and everyone just stood there, watching. No screaming, no excited chatter, no jumping up and down. Everyone was completely silent and still, as if unsure about what the proper etiquette was.

Wanting to give the queen the welcome that she deserved, I started to applaud. She walked down the red carpet, stopped at the hole where the tree was, took the spade, and shoveled some dirt into the hole. As I was at the very front of the tree, I took some great pictures with my cheap camera.

The queen then started to go around and meet the people who had worked in Kensington Gardens for years. She moved about the gardens gracefully and with an elegance that only true royalty could exude.

A line had formed. I went near the end of it, lingering behind the stanchions to wait until she was finished. Finally, she was standing very close to me, about seven to ten feet away. She was waiting for instructions on what to do next. Since nothing was happening, I felt compelled to contribute to the moment.

I opened my mouth wide and called out, "California loves you!"

The queen looked over at me and nodded politely.

Inspired by my comment, a guy called out, "Nebraska loves you too!"

Another nod from the queen.

Seeing the perfect opportunity, I opened my mouth yet again, boldly bringing the queen into a conversation. "Back home I work for Lucille Ball. And she said if I saw you to please say hello to you and your mum."

The muscles on the queen's face softened. "You know Lucille Ball?"

"Yes. And she really did say hello to you."

"Please tell her I say hello to her too. I love Lucy."

The guy from Nebraska took my camera and snapped a candid shot of me and the queen together. (Later on, I wondered if the queen would have posed if I had asked her to.)

A few minutes later, it was all over. She got back into her Rolls Royce and peeled away.

I left the gardens feeling invigorated by what had just occurred. I couldn't wait to pick up the phone and call Lucy.

But I had to wait. A whole four hours. That was when Wanda arrived at the office.

When the time came, I called, and Wanda connected me to Lucy. Eagerly I told her about my conversation with the queen and how she had said to say hello.

"The queen knew who I was?" Lucy asked, surprised.

When I came back to California, I couldn't wait to show Lucy the pictures of my trip to London, especially the one of me and the queen. After Lucy saw it, she demanded to have a copy of it. Gladly, I gave it to her, and she kept it in her house in a frame in the lanai room.

After Lucy passed away, Lucie gave me the framed picture.

CHAPTER 47

The day that Lucy showed me her old scrapbooks was the day that I truly got a glimpse into her past, into where she came from. She showed me pictures of her childhood home in Jamestown. As a theater in Jamestown was just about to be named after her, Lucy was getting ready to return there for the first time in years. Words could not describe how honored she was.

Arrangements were made for Lucy to stay at the Fenton Mansion.

"I'd be happier staying at the Holiday Inn," Lucy told me. There she would be able to just relax and see old friends. However, she was still immensely grateful for being invited to stay at the mansion.

As Lucy flipped through the pages of her scrapbooks, reminiscing about this story and that, I could tell that she was enjoying the stroll down memory lane. It was one of the first times I had ever heard her talk about her childhood days. She spoke about where she played, and about the stoop that she sat on for hours, just watching the neighbors. I felt privileged to be listening to all her stories.

During this time she was also in the midst of wardrobe fittings for the Sixty-First Academy Awards. She told me that she had picked out a heavy dress and hoped she had made the right choice. That year she was going to be a presenter with her good friend Bob Hope. After an introduction by Walter Matthau, they were both going to introduce a segment and announce the new stars of tomorrow.

"I'm nervous," Lucy confided in me.

I told Lucy that I was going to be a seat filler for the event and would see her there. A seat filler is one who keeps a seat warm whenever someone famous from the first ten to fifteen rows gets up and leaves, for any reason.

Not incredibly glamorous stuff, but at least I would be able to attend the big show.

Wearing my rented black tuxedo, I arrived at the ABC studios in Hollywood about six hours before the Oscar telecast. There were very strict rules that we were informed of upfront, among them, no autographs and no pictures. We were also told not to ask for a program, because after the show, we would be given one as a thank-you for being a seat filler.

Our badges were handed off to us. Badges that read "Seat Filler," the lowest of all the badges for the show. That meant that our freedom was highly compromised. First off, we couldn't go anywhere unescorted. Just about every area of the auditorium was off-limits to us. If we had to go to the bathroom, we had to negotiate for permission. We might as well have been in jail cells, for as seat fillers, we were truly the bottom of the barrel. But we were excited, nevertheless, to be at the Academy Awards, the most glamorous event in Hollywood.

The things I did for the sake of hobnobbing with the stars!

We boarded the bus to the Shrine Auditorium, where we went through the metal detectors. Next it was off to our post, which was down a long hallway. It felt like we were miles away from all the action. There wasn't much to see where we were, except for the floor, walls, and ceiling.

However, we were able to hear who was arriving from the loudspeakers that were outside.

Ladies and Gentlemen, Tom Hanks ...

Applause/screaming

Ladies and Gentlemen, Tom Cruise ...

Applause/screaming

The biggest cheer I heard was for Lucille Ball. That made me smile.

About ten minutes later, I walked over to the front door. Looking through it, I spotted Lucy and Gary, who were both decked out in the classiest of attire. They were walking on the red carpet, that forbidden place where no seat filler has ever been before.

Without even thinking about the consequences, I stepped out to say hello to them. I could have been thrown out right then and there, but no one was really watching the seat fillers. So I went for it.

I approached the stunning couple and made my presence known. Lucy, looking happy to see me, said, "Michael, get me inside. I have to go to the restroom."

Then she took my hand, and in we went.

It was like the *Here's Lucy* episode in which Lucy was being dragged by Richard Burton. Lucy Carter could care less about where she was being pulled to. In that moment, I felt the exact same way. We marched right to the backstage area. I didn't have the proper badge, but security wasn't in the least bit concerned.

I had Lucille Ball on my arm.

When we arrived at the green room, Lucy handed me her purse. "I'll be right back."

She headed off to the restroom, leaving Gary and me there to wait for her return. Minutes later, she came back to the green room and started chatting with her old friends, who were steadily making their entrances.

At one point, Lucy introduced me to the charismatic Jimmy Stewart.

"Michael, you know Jimmy Stewart," Lucy said, gesturing toward him. "We're neighbors."

She also introduced me to Cyd Charisse and Kim Hunter. I even saw her run into Geena Davis in the hallway and wish her well. Geena was up for Best Actress in a Supporting Role for *The Accidental Tourist* and actually went on to win later that night.

Fearing that someone would notice that one of the seat fillers was missing, I told Lucy and Gary I would try to see them after the show.

"I'm leaving right after my segment," Lucy told me. "Where are you sitting?"

"Somewhere in the first fifteen rows."

I checked my watch and saw that the show was about to begin.

I said good-bye to Lucy, and she leaned forward to give me a big kiss and hug.

She said, as she always did, "I love you."

I didn't know it then, but it would be the last time I would ever receive a hug from Lucy.

Hurrying back to my post, I slipped into the line. No one even noticed that I had left—and no one noticed that I had returned either. I told one of the guys in charge that Lucy and Gary would not be using their seats. He looked them up and then gave me permission to sit in Lucy's seat. It was in the second row. What luck.

When the show started, the announcer ran through the names of all the stars who were going to be appearing on the show that evening. I don't know if I was just biased, but it really seemed like Lucille Ball received the largest applause.

About an hour into the show, Walter Matthau stepped out onto the stage. I straightened my spine and tilted my head forward, preparing myself for a glimpse of my dear friend. After telling a few jokes, Walter Matthau graciously introduced Lucy and Bob Hope.

Within half a second, a sweeping version of the *I Love Lucy* theme song came gushing out of the orchestra. This was quickly followed by the Bob Hope "Thanks for the Memories" theme song.

I must have been the first one to hop to my feet and give Lucy and Bob a standing ovation. The applause was absolutely deafening. The audience's love for both Lucy and Bob was undeniable. It must have been a great feeling for them to hear their peers express such affection for them.

As Lucy reached the podium, she looked out and spotted me right away. We locked eyes.

She mouthed, "Hi, Mike."

A feeling of pure elation rushed through me. Lucy had just said hi to me at the Academy Awards.

Some of her last words to me were seen by almost a billion people.

Michelle Pfeiffer, who was sitting right next to me, asked, "Did she just say hello to you?"

"We're very close," I replied. "She's like a mother to me."

During their introduction of the new stars of tomorrow, Lucy and Bob demonstrated great chemistry, spontaneity, and enthusiasm. And when they finished up, Lucy was gone. Just like that.

She had done an amazing job. Although she hadn't been on television much in the last year, she acted as if she had not once taken a break from the spotlight. She was the ultimate pro. After a recent stroke, her health had been slowly declining. This information she kept private. She didn't want the public to feel sorry for her. Instead, Lucy wanted to keep moving forward, to keep things "business as usual." For in the eyes of her fans, she was a woman of strength and humor and exceptional talent. And even though her health was not perfect, she was still that woman. Seeing her onstage at the Academy Awards, I was more sure than I ever had been of that fact.

After the show ended, I did something that was against the rules—I collected autographs. There was absolutely no way I could resist. Without anyone catching me, I managed to get autographs from Tom Cruise, Tom Hanks, Dustin Hoffman, Geena Davis, and Melanie Griffith.

Fifteen minutes after the show had ended, the theater was just about empty. I got back onto the bus and headed toward ABC studios to get my car and the program I had been promised.

Before I left, the guy in charge nodded at me and said, "You did a good job." *If only he knew.*

*   *   *

A few days after the Academy Awards aired, I was on a national television program called *USA Today*, which was based on the newspaper. Wanda had given my name to the program when they were looking for someone to interview about Lucille Ball fans. It had been shot a few weeks before the day of the Academy Awards. The show had planned to interview Lucy as she walked down the red carpet; the reporters wanted to ask her questions about me and her fans in general. Since Lucy only walked down half the red carpet, they never got a chance to interview her.

After the show aired, I received a VHS tape of the *USA Today* program in the mail. I was eager for Lucy to see it, so I drove straight to her house. I bounded up the steps, rang the doorbell, and waited. After a few moments, Frank came to the door and let me inside.

I stepped in and saw that Lucy was napping peacefully on the sofa in the lanai room.

This would be the last time I would see her alive.

Not wanting to disturb Lucy, I gave Frank the tape and asked him to make sure she saw it.

A few days later, Lucy called me on the phone.

"You did wonderful for all the Lucy fans," she gushed. "You represented them so well. Thank you for being my number-one fan."

Hearing these words, I was very touched. Whenever Lucy said something, she meant it. I never took compliments lightly from her.

After a few minutes of chatting, we said good-bye to one another.

"I love you," said Lucy, before hanging up and ending our very last phone call together.

*   *   *

Days later, on April 18, news broke out on the radio and television that Lucy had suffered a heart attack. She was complaining of chest pains and had been rushed to the emergency room of Cedars-Sinai Medical Center. Press reports revealed that she was diagnosed as having a dissecting aortic aneurysm, and that she underwent surgery for close to eight hours. The surgery was successful. And beyond that, there was no more information.

When I heard the news, my entire being was gripped with extreme panic. I tried like crazy to get in touch with Wanda, but it was very difficult that day. I was in the dark about Lucy's condition, just as everyone else was.

Over the next ten days, the media was saturated with news on Lucy and her health. Banners lined the street across from Lucy's window. Words like "Get well, Lucy" and "We love you, Lucy" were written in markers and paint for all to see. Fans from every part of the world donated blood in her name. Thousands and thousands of "get well" letters flooded the hospital. It was the largest amount of mail that any person had ever received at Cedars-Sinai.

When I finally got through to Wanda, she told me that no one could see Lucy at that time except for immediate family. I completely understood that it wasn't my place.

All I could do was pray.

The first time I saw Lucy in person was at the Here's Lucy
filming on October 28, 1971, with guest star Bob Cummings...

*...and the last time I saw her on stage was on March 29,
1989 at the 61st Academy Awards with Bob Hope*

*   *   *

More days passed. News reports were full of words that pointed toward Lucy being on the mend. She was *getting better*.

On April 24, Lucy was supposed to appear at the Beverly Hills Hotel to receive the Eastman Kodak Second Century Award. The organizers were leaning toward canceling the event, but Lucie jumped in and agreed to accept the award on her mother's behalf.

In speaking to the press, Lucie said that her mother was doing better and that the get well cards were coming in by the truckload. She said that Lucy was ready to come home and get on with her life.

At the award ceremony, Lucy's dear friend Carol Burnett was present. Taking to the stage, Carol told the same story about how they had met at the second performance of *Once upon a Mattress*. Only this time, it was different. It was tinged with a deep ache, with sadness. It sounded as if she was going to cry.

Maybe she knew more about Lucy's condition than we were led to believe?

The tribute to Lucy was full of such love. It was a sweet and wonderful night, one that made me miss my dear friend even more.

Lucie came up to me and said, "I saw you on a couple of shows, and I was very touched by the things you were saying about my mom." She paused to take a breath and then smiled. "She's ready to come home and play backgammon with you again soon."

*   *   *

On April 26, 1989, I received a phone call a little after 6:00 a.m. It was my friend Barbara Awerkamp. Right away I knew something was wrong. Her tone was low and strained.

In the most gentle way possible, Barbara said words that delivered a crushing blow to my senses: "I just heard on the radio that Lucy passed away."

I was stunned. The day before Wanda had told me that Lucy was doing better and would get to go home in a few days. My heart dropped all the way down into my stomach as I struggled to understand what I had just been told. It was as if the ground had been ripped out from underneath me.

"Should I come over?" Barbara asked, sensing my shock.

"I'll be okay," I said. "I just want to be alone."

Within five minutes, Wanda called and, in a shaky voice, told me the news as well. We were both in tears.

Unable to restrain our emotion, we both broke down together, expressing the tremendous loss we had just been struck with. We consoled one another, trying to find comfort in sharing our grief.

For years Lucy had always been there. Supporting me, encouraging me, accepting me. To imagine my life without her was simply impossible.

After hanging up with Wanda, the producer of *Entertainment Tonight* called to tell me the news. I had met her when she was working on the *USA Today* shoot that I had done just a month earlier. She wanted to know if a crew could come by and get a comment from me.

At first I told her I was in no mood to talk, but after a couple of minutes went by, I agreed.

By 8:00 a.m., the crew was at my house, ready to record.

Wanda gave my number out to other press people as well, just in case they wanted to talk to a friend or a fan.

My brother-in-law's sister, Marilyn, came over and started answering the phone for me. She knew that I needed someone there. By the end of the night, she had logged over 175 phone calls. Every relative, friend, and acquaintance I had ever met called to wish me their condolences. Not only that, but just about every television station called me.

Can you give us a comment and talk to the CBS Morning Show?
Can you talk to Dan Rather's office?

It became a challenge to navigate all the requests. I learned that if I talked to the *Today* show, I wasn't allowed to talk to *Good Morning America*. Balancing everything got to be quite a headache. With all the distractions, I had no time to mourn for the entire day.

The only time I broke down was at 9:00 a.m., right before *I Love Lucy* was to air at its regular time. Right before the show, a newscaster said, "What a tribute it is that we can watch her right now!"

Words came up on the screen—"LUCILLE BALL 1911–1989."

And that's what did it for me. I completely lost it. My cup ran over with the utmost sadness, grief, and pain. This was final. There was no turning back from this. I would never see my friend again. Never hear her deep and contagious laughter, never feel the warmth of her hugs, never delight in the presence of her company. At the age of seventy-seven, she was gone. Just like that. Those words on the television screen marked the end of an era. The end of a sweet and precious time.

*   *   *

I was set to be on *Good Morning America* the next morning. The show had planned to pick me up in a limo at 2:00 a.m. and take me to the ABC studios in Hollywood for a live remote.

At 11:00 p.m. the night before, I received the last of my phone calls of the night. *Good Morning America* had canceled me. The show had gotten a hold of "Little Ricky," Keith Thibodeaux, and I was out.

But that didn't matter. A few hours later I was in a car headed to ABC studios to do the local talk show, *A.M. Los Angeles*. Steve Edwards and Christina Ferrare were the hosts of the show. They spent the whole hour talking about Lucy. Phyllis Diller, Mary Wickes, Larry Anderson, and James Bacon came on to talk about the person that Lucy had been. Mary told a story about how she and Lucy came to visit me at the May Company. It was amazing to hear everyone's stories.

Looking back, I can't believe any of us were ready to talk less than twenty-four hours after her death. Maybe it was healthy for us to do it that way. No doubt, Lucy would have wanted it to go down exactly as it did. She would have wanted us to stay strong in the face of all the sadness we felt.

When I got home, Gary called and told me he had seen me the day before on *Entertainment Tonight* and *AM Los Angeles*.

"You've been saying some very nice things. I'm proud of you. Lucy would have been touched," Gary told me. "She thought you were a very special young man."

That same day I headed off to the FOX station in Los Angeles (that aired the *I Love Lucy* program) to talk to the head of programming. He told me that the network was planning to show complete coverage of Lucy's funeral, something I knew Lucy would have hated. She wouldn't have wanted a circus-type of service. She would have just wanted family.

And that was exactly what she got.

Her service ended up being an intimate one, with only Gary, Lucie, and Desi in attendance. It was held early in the morning at the Forest Lawn Memorial Park in the Hollywood Hills next to Universal Studios.

Lucy was cremated and placed next to her mom, DeDe. American flags all over the city were at half mast. The television capital of the world had lost its queen. There were signs on billboards that read, "Rest In Peace, Lucy."

FOX still wanted to do something to honor the life of Lucy. The network put together an all-day, commercial-free *I Love Lucy* marathon. Many of Lucy's friends dropped by to speak between the shows—Bob Carroll Jr., Madelyn Pugh Davis, Shirley Mitchell, Doris Singleton, Elvia Allman, Lou Krugman, Maurice Marsac, Larry Anderson, Ann Dusenberry, Vicki Lawrence, Tom Watson, and Bart Andrews. It was a day of celebration. A day to wipe away the tears and laugh. To pay tribute to a remarkable woman.

On *The Arsenio Hall Show*, Lucie made a beautiful comment about her mother, saying that Lucille Ball had passed away and would be mourned forever, but that Lucy Ricardo was still very much alive.

"We should not forget that," Lucie said.

Lucy will make us laugh forever. And what an honor for her to be remembered by laughter.

During the weeks that followed, support flooded to me from every direction. People kept coming up to me and wishing me well. I received over two hundred cards and flowers from other fans, who were all around the world. Everyone seemed to know that I was in mourning. People would come up to my table if I was at a restaurant. And since my personalized license plate read "1lcyfan," it was easy for anyone to spot me on a road full of cars. People would honk their horns at me, to let me know that they, too, loved Lucy. The support was pouring in from ever direction.

We all had just lost a good friend— one who had been in our homes every day for nearly four decades.

On the AM Los Angeles set (L-R) me, Larry Anderson, Phyllis Diller, James Bacon, Mary Wickes, Steve Edwards, and Christina Ferrari

CHAPTER 48

On May 8, 1989, Lucie thought it would be nice to hold a memorial service for the fans across the nation. The outpouring of love for her mother was tremendous. Ever since the day we lost Lucy, a cloud had been cast over the world. Her absence was deeply felt. Fans needed desperately to say good-bye, needed a way to get closure of some sort, to come together and heal.

Lucie planned for three services, all on Monday night, starting at 8:00 p.m.—the same time that all of Lucy's CBS series had aired.

Monday night was Lucy's night. And it would always be her night.

The services were held in New York, Chicago, and Los Angeles.

The Los Angeles service was held in Santa Monica at the St. Monica's Catholic Church. Over two thousand people attended the service. I arrived early, and as soon as I got there, I was told to go to a private area of the church where Lucie and her husband Larry Luckinbill, were talking to the Reverend Robert Schuller about the upcoming service. It was the first time that I had seen any of the family since Lucy's passing.

A wellspring of emotion filled my chest. I threw my arms around Lucie, and we held each other for a moment.

"Everything's going to be okay," Lucie whispered. "Know that she loved you."

After we pulled apart, Lucie told me that after the service, a few close friends were getting together at her house for some food and drinks. She wanted me to come too. My heart softened at hearing her invitation. It was so nice of her to ask me to be there.

I went to the front of the church, where I greeted just about everyone. Dozens upon dozens of people approached me, telling me how sorry they were. Everyone knew that I had lost one of my best friends. The love and support that was flowing toward me was so amazingly overwhelming.

I kept looking for Wanda. She was coming from work, and I wanted to save her a seat next to me.

But she could not be found.

I finally went outside and saw Wanda among a crowd of about five hundred people who couldn't get into the church.

I approached the guard. "Please let her in."

And just like that, Wanda was by my side, and we were making our way into the church.

I sat in the front, right next to Wanda, Lucie, and Carol Burnett. The Reverend Robert Schuller talked about his family and his love for Lucy. He told us a story about how, after one of his services, his family had gone home and popped in a VCR tape. Settling back in his chair, he had nodded his head, proud of his family. He figured they were putting in a tape of one of his sermons.

But, nope.

It was a tape of *I Love Lucy*.

The roomful of people in the church chuckled.

"Lucy was the gift of humor," Schuller went on to say. "Let's applaud the Lord for Lucille Ball."

The two-thousand-plus attendants stood up and gave Lucy a two-minute standing ovation that was one of the most deafening standing ovations I had heard. It was so loud that I thought the roof was going to cave in. As the thunderous applause overtook my senses, tears fell from my eyes. They weren't coming from a place of sadness. They were rooted in happiness, in knowing that the world still loved Lucy—and did so with tremendous passion.

After the service, we headed to Lucie and Larry's home in Santa Monica. There were only about twenty of us there. We gave Lucy a loving toast and spent all evening talking about the person she was. Completely transfixed by all the words that were being said about Lucy, I did most of the listening.

Thelma Orloff said to me, "Lucy was very blessed to know you. She thought of you as a son."

Lucie's oldest son, around seven years old, drew a picture of a rocket and said, in a small and innocent voice, "Nana is off to heaven now."

Without warning, the pressure of emotion filled my chest. And then the tears started coming, all over again.

CHAPTER 49

Although no one can ever replace Lucy's spot inside my heart, I've made some other special friends along the way.

One of my favorite shows of all time is *The Brady Bunch*. It was the show to watch when I was in elementary school. Just about every kid could relate to one of the Brady kids. You were either the oldest child, the middle child, or the youngest child of a family. (And if you were an only child, you watched *The Brady Bunch* wishing you could be part of a large family as fun and loving as their family was.) Since I was the youngest in my family, I related mostly to Bobby Brady.

About twelve years ago, I started working on an award show called *The Victors*, which honors athletes in all fields. *The Victors* took place in Las Vegas, at the Las Vegas Hilton Hotel. It was an event that I loved working on. Not only did I get a free week in Las Vegas, but we were also allowed to sign our names to anything we wanted at the Hilton.

Each year that I worked on the award show, a slew of Hollywood stars and sports figures would come and also stay at the hotel. Some of the celebrities who attended were Dyan Cannon, Estelle Getty, Fran Drescher, Jimmy Kimmel, Vanna White, Yogi Berra, Shaquille O'Neal, Mark Spitz, and Bruce Jenner. Another athlete guest was Mitch Gaylord, an old friend of mine from elementary school and high school. Mitch was a gymnast and a four-time medal winner at the 1984 Olympics.

There was one celebrity who never missed *The Victors*—Florence Henderson, the bright and bubbly mom from *The Brady Bunch*. Florence was a huge supporter of the award show because all the proceeds went to her favorite charity, the City of Hope hospital in California. It's one of the largest medical facilities that is committed to the treatment and research of cancer.

The first time I met Florence, I fell in love with her right away. She is exactly what you would think she'd be—sweet, charming, and wonderful. Very much like the Carol Brady she portrayed on television for years. She's a caring and personable woman, someone who takes the time to know you, even if you're just getting an autograph from her.

During one of my stints working for *The Victors*, I was hanging out in the lobby, about to go to another hotel to meet my parents for dinner. I crossed paths with Florence and told her where I was off to. Then we parted ways, and I headed out to meet my parents.

Well, about ninety minutes later, I came back to the Las Vegas Hilton. Florence was out by the slot machines.

"How was your dinner?" she asked me.

"My parents stood me up."

I had gone to their hotel and couldn't find them anywhere. They weren't answering their cell phones. I checked every restaurant at the hotel—twice. Well, every restaurant except for the buffet. My dad always hated buffets, so I figured they wouldn't be anywhere near there.

However, you guessed it … I discovered later that they were at the buffet. I had completely missed them.

Upon hearing of my failed dinner plans, Florence looked me straight in the eye and said, "Then you're coming with me. You'll have dinner with us."

The invitation was one I could simply not refuse.

That night I had dinner with Florence, her husband, John, and a few of her friends. We ate in the private dining room at a steakhouse. And thanks to Lucy, I remembered to order my steak butterflied.

During dinner, Florence and I traded Lucy stories, sharing our most wonderful memories. Florence told me that she had never appeared with Lucy on television, but many times they would be at the same fund-raisers and special events.

The next morning we came down to the lobby at the same time for breakfast. Once again, we ate together, delighting in one another's company.

One of the highlights of my yearly trip to Vegas was seeing Florence. Almost every year, she brought her daughter Barbara with her. Barbara is every bit as wonderful as her mom.

During one of my trips, Florence taught me how to play the slots.

"You don't need to rush," she would tell me. "Just put the quarters in one at a time, but always play the maximum on the slot machine."

Now it's all done with paper. No more coins into the slots.

Although I no longer work *The Victors*, Florence and I run into each other a few times a year, either at other charity events or at one of her nightclub acts. She's a terrific performer, full of openness and charisma. She's an extraordinary storyteller and singer. I've seen her perform on both the East Coast and the West Coast. We even exchange holiday cards each year. She has become a very good friend.

Recently, Florence appeared on *Dancing with the Stars*. If that isn't proof enough that she can do just about anything she sets her mind to, I don't know what is. With grace, determination, and skill, she danced her way into the hearts of many. I was fortunate enough to attend all of her beautiful performances. Florence will always be a winner in my eyes.

I really think I have a knack for picking wonderful and special people to populate my life. I'm very lucky in that regard!

Placing my hands in cement at the Lucy-Desi Center in Jamestown, New York

(L-R) me, Carole Cook, Wanda Clark, Tom Troupe, and Lucie Arnaz

Meeting Queen Elizabeth of England

Playing Lucy slots with Florence Henderson

With Betty White backstage during a taping of Super Password

*With Betty White and Florence Henderson at a luncheon
honoring game shows (photo by Rick Carl)*

CHAPTER 50

Lucy once gave me an envelope with one hundred autographed pictures that she had signed for me.

"Save them," she told me. "One day you'll need these."

I had no clue what she meant.

Many years later, I understood. Somehow she knew what the future had in store for me.

In the years after Lucy's death, my Lucy collection has continued to flourish. It doesn't matter whether it's an old or new item, my excitement for growing my collection is immense.

I own just about everything imaginable. All of the *I Love Lucy* comic books, including all five of *The Lucy Show* comic books. I'm also the proud owner of every Lucy doll ever made (and no, that's not an exaggeration), from the 1953 *I Love Lucy* rag doll to the Madame Alexander, Franklin Mint, and Mattel dolls.

My *Lucy and Ricky and Fred and Ethel* book has been signed by over sixty-five people who either appeared or worked on *I Love Lucy*. Among these autographs are ones from guests stars like Barbara Eden, who played Diana Jordan in the "Country Club Dance" episode; Aaron Spelling, who played Gas Station Man in the "Tennessee Bound" episode; Natalie Schafer, who played Phoebe Emerson in "The Charm School" episode; Elvia Allman, who played The Factory Foreman in the "Job Switching" episode; and June Foray, who played the voice of Fred the Dog in the "Little Ricky Gets a Dog" episode.

Who will be next?

I also have Jess Oppenheimer's signature, thanks to his son Gregg Oppenheimer. And thanks to eBay, I have been lucky enough to find the autographs of Kathryn Card (Mrs. McGillicuddy), Bobby Jellison (Bobby the Bellboy), Elizabeth Patterson (Mrs. Trumbull), and Mabel Paige (Mrs. Hansen).

I own thousands of Lucy-related items, and I don't have any plans to stop growing my collection any time soon.

*   *   *

Now, twenty years after Lucy's death, I'm working on the hit talk show *Dr. Phil* as the audience supervisor. I've been with the show since its fourth season. Along with my staff, I'm responsible for making sure that the audience arrives on time. I also seat the crowd and work to keep them comfortable and happy. Dr. Phil takes care of the rest.

A true professional, he is great about not keeping the audience waiting. His shows *always* start on time, no matter what. Dr. Phil is 100 percent aware of the audience and treats audience members as if they were guests in his own home, something that Lucy also did during her tapings.

Lucy and Dr. Phil are very similar. Not only does Dr. Phil care about his guests, as Lucy did, but he also wants nothing but the best show possible. Lucy was always that way, giving every single project her all. Dr. Phil knows exactly what he wants and is willing to work hard for it. It always has to be the best possible product. If it isn't, then why bother putting the energy into it in the first place?

Working on Dr. Phil's show has been one of the most enjoyable experiences of my life. I love telling the audience that the studio they're in was once RKO Studios. That in 1940, Lucy and Desi first met, right there on Stage Twenty-Nine to film the movie *Too Many Girls*. And eighteen years later, they bought the studio and named it Desilu. Now it is known as Paramount Studios.

I can't help but think that Lucy is looking down on me, proud to see me doing the job I always wanted to do, the job that I was meant for. You know you must be doing something you love when you're eager to get out of bed and to work each morning.

The best part of my job is that I get to greet each and every audience member who comes to the show. As an audience member myself for forty years, I'm sensitive to making sure that everyone is having a great time, and that everyone feels welcomed. There's nothing that thrills me more than to know that all our guests are happy.

I was ecstatic the day that Lucie came to visit me and Dr. Phil for an episode. It was in February of 2007. Lucie had not been to Paramount Studios for a very long time. She took a tour around the lot and was so happy to see that the studio had named a park and a building after Lucy. And, of course, Lucy's old bungalow also bears her name on it.

Sometimes I'll stop and reflect on everything ... and it's mind-blowing to see how it all adds up. If you think about it, what are the odds that I would be here, two decades after Lucy has left this planet? That I would be working on the studio lot where Desilu was once located? The place where Lucy and Desi met and started their journey of revolutionizing television together. The place where Lucy's name is etched into different plaques.

Destiny is a funny thing.

(L-R) me, Lucie Arnaz, Dr. Phil and Robin McGraw the day Lucie came to visit us at a taping of the Dr. Phil Show. It is the same RKO Studio stage where Lucy & Desi first met in 1940

Lucy & Desi on Gower Street, the same entrance that I use every day for the Dr. Phil Show *at Paramount Studios. It was once home to RKO and Desilu Studios*

EPILOGUE

It took me a long time to realize that Lucy was a big star. Don't take me for a fool—I knew she was famous. But never did I imagine that she was eternally famous. That all the work she left behind would continue to be admired today, over twenty years after her passing. That her comedic genius would persist through the decades, bringing laughter to generation after generation that comes upon it.

Since her death, the entire world has been honoring the legacy of Lucille Ball in countless ways. The television academy unveiled a life-sized statue of Lucy blowing a kiss. In Palm Springs, there's a full-sized statue of Lucy sitting on a park bench. Special awards have been given to her posthumously by the Women in Film and the TV Land Awards, among other organizations. Hollywood and Florida had a tribute dedicated to Lucy's amazing career. Even the Franklin Mint in Philadelphia had an exhibit. There was also a fiftieth anniversary road tour of *I Love Lucy* that crossed the country. And not only did the United States Post Office carry a stamp of Lucy, there are Lucy conventions all over the world that still honor her today.

Lucille Ball was a star to many. She was a special lady who demonstrated exceptional prowess in the field of entertainment. With grace, courage, and humor, Lucy set the world on fire, brought laughter and freedom to the face of television in a way that no one ever had before.

I am so honored that she graced my life with her friendship.

Not a day goes by that I don't miss her. That I don't wish to call her on the phone and tell her what's on my mind, that I don't have the urge to swing by for a quick game of backgammon.

Lucy, I miss you with all my heart.

And I'm proud to be your number-one fan …

Then, now, and forever.

Please check out my web site at TheLucyFan.com
Or write to me at
Michael Stern
P.O. Box 280684
Northridge, CA 91328-0684